OpenStack® Cloud
Application Development

Scott Adkins
John Belamaric
Vincent Giersch
Denys Makogon
Jason Robinson

wrox™

A Wiley Brand

OpenStack® Cloud Application Development

Published by
John Wiley & Sons, Inc.
10475 Crosspoint Boulevard
Indianapolis, IN 46256
www.wiley.com

Copyright © 2016 by John Wiley & Sons, Inc., Indianapolis, Indiana

Published simultaneously in Canada

ISBN: 978-1-119-19431-6

ISBN: 978-1-119-23964-2 (ebk)

ISBN: 978-1-119-19434-7 (ebk)

Manufactured in the United States of America

10 9 8 7 6 5 4 3 2 1

For general information on our other products and services please contact our Customer Care Department within the United States at (877) 762-2974, outside the United States at (317) 572-3993 or fax (317) 572-4002.

Wiley publishes in a variety of print and electronic formats and by print-on-demand. Some material included with standard print versions of this book may not be included in e-books or in print-on-demand. If this book refers to media such as a CD or DVD that is not included in the version you purchased, you may download this material at http://booksupport.wiley.com. For more information about Wiley products, visit www.wiley.com.

Library of Congress Control Number: 2015953113

ABOUT THE AUTHORS

 SCOTT ADKINS is a technical lead for the Cloud Operations team at Comcast. He helps the team deploy new internal OpenStack environments, as well as helping onboard other teams into the cloud. In particular, Scott helps newcomers to the cloud understand the pet versus cattle model and how their applications can be adjusted to run more effectively in the OpenStack cloud environment. Scott has been a UNIX and Linux Systems Administrator for more than 30 years. Prior to his work at Comcast, he was a technical lead at Savvis Communications for the UNIX team. Scott lives in Leesburg, Virginia with his wife and four children.

 JOHN BELAMARIC is a software and systems architect with nearly 20 years of software design and development experience. His current focus is on cloud network automation. He is a key architect of the Infoblox Cloud products, concentrating on OpenStack integration and development. He brings to this his experience as the lead architect for the Infoblox Network Automation product line, along with a wealth of networking, network management, software, and product design knowledge. He is a contributor to both the OpenStack Neutron and Designate projects. He lives in Bethesda, Maryland with his wife Robin and two children, Owen and Audrey.

 VINCENT GIERSCH is the co-founder and CTO of Flat.io, where he mainly works on the automation of deployment and scaling of the SaaS application. Prior to that, at the University of Kent and in partnership with JANET, he designed and implemented the support of the IETF ABFAB (Application Bridging for Federated Access Beyond Web) in OpenStack Keystone to provide a non-web federated authentication. Recently he worked as an R&D Platform Engineer at OVH.com, developing a Docker hosting platform based on OpenStack. He is from Nantes, France.

 DENYS MAKOGON is a developer and software architect of cloud platforms, mainly focused on developing and designing platform and Software-as-a-Service applications for OpenStack. He is a lead software developer for Gigaspaces, concentrating on Cloudify product development along with bringing well-designed and production-ready integration with VMware cloud platforms, including vCloud Air. He is a contributor to the OpenStack DBaaS platform and OpenStack CloudValidation open source framework. He lives in Kharkiv, Ukraine.

JASON ROBINSON is a senior platform developer at GoDaddy. He helps teams transition traditional applications to their internal OpenStack cloud with a focus on orchestration and resiliency. Prior to his work with OpenStack, he was an architect on GoDaddy's cloud storage product and a principal developer of their webmail offering.

Jason has been working as a professional web developer for 18 years, and in addition to serving as a lead engineer for tech-centered companies like GoDaddy, Verizon, and GTE, he has done extensive work in the fields of e-commerce, telemedicine, and streaming media. When not pursuing the perfectly scalable application, Jason is an avid runner, maker, amateur philosopher, and most recently a father.

ABOUT THE TECHNICAL EDITORS

CHRIS DENT, Senior Software Engineer at Red Hat, primarily focuses on improving, integrating, and testing OpenStack. Prior to Red Hat he worked as a freelance consultant designing and developing HTTP APIs for collaborative document systems.

LARS BUTLER is a core engineer for ZeroVM and led the project's mini design summit at OpenStack Summit Atlanta. His previous F/OSS work includes OpenQuake Engine, a scalable distributed calculation engine for computing global earthquake hazard and risk, developed in collaboration with the Swiss Seismological Service.

JOE TALERICO, Performance Engineer at Red Hat, is a seasoned Senior Computer Engineer experienced in integrating leading edge technologies into existing infrastructures. He has developed solutions and automation frameworks around technologies ranging from Cloud, Virtualization, Storage, End User Computing, Unified Communications, Datacenter, IPTV, and Android.

CREDITS

PROJECT EDITOR
Charlotte Kughen

TECHNICAL EDITORS
Chris Dent, Lars Butler, Joe Talerico

PRODUCTION EDITOR
Christine O'Connor

COPYEDITOR
Christina Rudloff

**MANAGER OF CONTENT DEVELOPMENT
& ASSEMBLY**
Mary Beth Wakefield

PRODUCTION MANAGER
Kathleen Wisor

MARKETING DIRECTOR
David Mayhew

**PROFESSIONAL TECHNOLOGY &
STRATEGY DIRECTOR**
Barry Pruett

BUSINESS MANAGER
Amy Knies

ASSOCIATE PUBLISHER
Jim Minatel

PROJECT COORDINATOR, COVER
Brent Savage

PROOFREADER
Christina Rudloff

INDEXER
Robert Swanson

COVER DESIGNER
Wiley

COVER IMAGE
Alexandra Lande/Shutterstock

ACKNOWLEDGMENTS

I would like to thank my wife and children for their patience and support while I worked on this project. I would like to also thank the OpenStack community for everything they do to build upon and support the open source cloud. Without the OpenStack community, we would not have the cloud platform we have today!

—SCOTT ADKINS

I would like to thank my wife and children for their support and encouragement throughout this project.

—JOHN BELAMARIC

I would like to thank the entire team, who helped me to complete this project and gave the appropriate level of support, and my family, who helped me to stay focused on this book.

—DENYS MAKOGON

I would like to thank my wife Tara who took care of all of us while I was working on this book, my brother for giving me my first computer and, of course, my parents, who supported me even when I decided to pursue a philosophy degree (every parent's worst nightmare).

—JASON ROBINSON

CONTENTS

PART II: DEVELOPING AND DEPLOYING APPLICATIONS WITH OPENSTACK

INTRODUCTION

OPENSTACK IS A SET OF SOFTWARE PACKAGES THAT MANAGE virtualized resources, including computing, networking, and storage. It enables you to create and destroy virtual machines, connect them together with private networks, provide network-based storage, and make them available to the rest of your network and the world. OpenStack provides consistent, uniform API services for all of this, hiding hypervisor and vendor specific details from the applications that are using the APIs. It also provides a user interface, built on top of the same APIs, that allows users to see and manage their virtual resources.

WHO THIS BOOK IS FOR

This book is for application developers that are interested in learning more about OpenStack and how it will transform the application design and development process. It is for someone who is new to the cloud environment, who wants a broad understanding of that environment, as well as a deep enough knowledge to make practical use of OpenStack.

WHAT THIS BOOK COVERS

This book will provide a broad understanding of cloud concepts and how they fit into the life of an application developer. It will drill in deeply to the OpenStack services that are most important to an application developer, and show you how these services will change not only how you deploy applications, but also how you design them. It will provide detailed information on each service, and provide examples of how each service may be used by an application developer.

HOW THIS BOOK IS STRUCTURED

This book was written in two parts. Part 1 provides an overview of OpenStack. The purpose of this part is to lay the groundwork, covering all of the OpenStack technologies and what is most important.

Part 2 takes the reader through developing and deploying applications with OpenStack. In this part you will build an example on top of OpenStack that drills down much deeper on the technologies, provides tips, and helps you learn about OpenStack through the lens of these same technologies.

Here is a list of the chapters:

➤ Part I: OpenStack Overview

    ➤ Chapter 1: Introduction to OpenStack

    ➤ Chapter 2: Understanding the OpenStack Ecosystem: Core Projects

    ➤ Chapter 3: Understanding the OpenStack Ecosystem: Additional Projects

WHAT YOU NEED TO USE THIS BOOK

You should understand the basics of application development - how applications are composed of multiple servers like web servers, application servers, and database servers. You do not need any cloud-specific knowledge, though you should be aware of what virtualization and virtual machines are, and have a basic understanding of networks.

CONVENTIONS

To help you get the most from the text and keep track of what's happening, we've used a number of conventions throughout the book.

Examples that you can download and try out for yourself generally appear in a box like this:

EXAMPLE TITLE

This section gives a brief overview of the example.

Source

This section includes the source code.

```
Source code
Source code
Source code
```

Output

This section lists the output:

```
Example output
Example output
Example output
```

> **NOTE** *Notes indicates notes, tips, hints, tricks, or and asides to the current discussion.*

As for styles in the text:

➤ *We* highlight *new terms and important words when we introduce them.*

➤ *We show code within the text like so:* `persistence.properties`.

SOURCE CODE

As you work through the examples in this book, you may choose either to type in all the code manually, or to use the source code files that accompany the book. All the source code used in this book is available for download at `www.wrox.com`. Specifically for this book, the code download is on the Download Code tab at:

`www.wrox.com/go/openstackcloudappdev`

and at:

`https://github.com/johnbelamaric/openstack-appdev-book`

You can also search for the book at `www.wrox.com` by ISBN (the ISBN for this book is 978-1-119-19431-6) to find the code. And a complete list of code downloads for all current Wrox books is available at `www.wrox.com/dynamic/books/download.aspx`.

> **NOTE** *Because many books have similar titles, you may find it easiest to search by ISBN; this book's ISBN is 978-1-119-19431-6.*

Once you download the code, just decompress it with your favorite compression tool. Alternately, you can go to the main Wrox code download page at `www.wrox.com/dynamic/books/download.aspx` to see the code available for this book and all other Wrox books.

ERRATA

We make every effort to ensure that there are no errors in the text or in the code. However, no one is perfect, and mistakes do occur. If you find an error in one of our books, like a spelling mistake or faulty piece of code, we would be very grateful for your feedback. By sending in errata, you may save another reader hours of frustration, and at the same time, you will be helping us provide even higher quality information.

To find the errata page for this book, go to

`www.wrox.com/go/openstackcloudappdev`

And click the Errata link. On this page you can view all errata that has been submitted for this book and posted by Wrox editors.

If you don't spot "your" error on the Book Errata page, go to www.wrox.com/contact/ techsupport.shtml and complete the form there to send us the error you have found. We'll check the information and, if appropriate, post a message to the book's errata page and fix the problem in subsequent editions of the book.

P2P.WROX.COM

For author and peer discussion, join the P2P forums at http://p2p.wrox.com. The forums are a Web-based system for you to post messages relating to Wrox books and related technologies and interact with other readers and technology users. The forums offer a subscription feature to e-mail you topics of interest of your choosing when new posts are made to the forums. Wrox authors, editors, other industry experts, and your fellow readers are present on these forums.

At http://p2p.wrox.com, you will find a number of different forums that will help you, not only as you read this book, but also as you develop your own applications. To join the forums, just follow these steps:

1. Go to http://p2p.wrox.com and click the Register link.
2. Read the terms of use and click Agree.
3. Complete the required information to join, as well as any optional information you wish to provide, and click Submit.
4. You will receive an e-mail with information describing how to verify your account and complete the joining process.

> **NOTE** *You can read messages in the forums without joining P2P, but in order to post your own messages, you must join.*

Once you join, you can post new messages and respond to messages other users post. You can read messages at any time on the Web. If you would like to have new messages from a particular forum e-mailed to you, click the Subscribe to this Forum icon by the forum name in the forum listing.

For more information about how to use the Wrox P2P, be sure to read the P2P FAQs for answers to questions about how the forum software works, as well as many common questions specific to P2P and Wrox books. To read the FAQs, click the FAQ link on any P2P page.

PART I
OpenStack Overview

Introducing OpenStack

WHAT'S IN THIS CHAPTER?

➤   Models of cloud computing

➤   Relevance of cloud computing to application developers

➤   Why OpenStack is a good cloud platform choice

➤   How OpenStack is put together

WHAT IS CLOUD COMPUTING?

There is so much hype around cloud computing that it is often difficult to get a clear sense of what anyone means by those words. Is it just virtualization? Is it *Software-as-a-Service* (*SaaS*), such as Microsoft's Office 365 and Salesforce.com? Or is it the ability to get a virtual machine instantly from Amazon Web Services (AWS) or Azure? And what about online storage such as Dropbox?

Types of Cloud Computing

The reality is that cloud computing refers to all of these things just described and more. The National Institute of Standards and Technology (NIST) has come up with an "official" definition based upon five key components: on-demand self-service, broad network access, pooled resources, elasticity, and metered service. In general, these characteristics may be provided in several different models. These models help sort out the confusion and hype. In fact, these can be thought of as layers in a stack, with each layer being built on top of the previous one (see Figure 1-1).

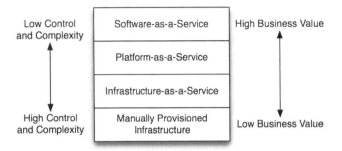

FIGURE 1-1

In Figure 1-1, "Manually Provisioned Infrastructure" represents the traditional method of building your information technology infrastructure—this is not cloud computing. In this environment, physical machines are racked, connected, and configured on a one-by-one basis. This provides complete control, but requires substantial time and effort to build out, or to change when necessary. Of course, all clouds need to run on physical gear at some point, so this provides the basic foundation for everything else. One of the keys to making cloud computing successful, however, is to move the complexity out of this layer and up higher in the stack.

Infrastructure-as-a-Service (IaaS) is the most basic layer in the cloud computing stack. This is OpenStack's primary focus, as well as the primary focus for AWS. It enables automated or self-service provisioning of compute, networking, and storage. Typically, these resources are provided as Virtual Machines (VMs), but you could also use it to spin up bare metal servers (i.e. physical hosts). This is known as "Metal-as-a-Service," and OpenStack provides a project for managing this service as well. Alternatively, you can also spin up containers rather than VMs or bare metal servers. The essential point is that it enables the provisioning of compute instances, with (optionally) attached networking and storage.

Platform-as-a-Service (PaaS) builds on top of IaaS to enable the provisioning of applications, rather than simply the infrastructure that might be used to run the application. So, a PaaS provides core common services needed by applications, along with the machinery to configure and deploy applications to use those services. A PaaS typically will provide a complete application stack (web server, application server, database server, etc.) into which you can easily deploy your application. Heroku (`https://www.heroku.com`) is an example of a popular PaaS for applications built with a variety of standard frameworks, such as Ruby-on-Rails. With Heroku you can deploy your application to the Internet with a simple `git push`. As the application author and deployer, you don't need to worry about configuring and deploying the different tiers, or even worry about how to scale them. If you follow the Heroku conventions, everything is handled by the PaaS.

Software-as-a-Service (SaaS) is the layer farthest from the underlying physical infrastructure. It may be built on IaaS or a PaaS, but need not be—the point is the user never really knows. This is the simplest form of cloud computing from the point of view of the user because they have no insight into the actual mechanics or systems behind the service. It's just a service they use. Often this is provided in the form of a website, such as Salesforce.com. But you can also get lower-level services such as Database-as-a-Service, where you simply request via an API (or website) for a database with certain parameters, and are given an IP and port to connect to. As a user of the service, you don't need to worry about how to scale that service—though you will need to pay more as your use of the service increases.

Put succinctly, IaaS provides the tools to "build" your systems from the ground up. PaaS allows you to "deploy" your applications, without needing to worry about the underlying infrastructure. SaaS allows you to "buy" your applications—you do not even need to deploy or manage them at all. This is a steady progression of decreasing control and complexity, while increasing direct business value.

While these are general models for cloud computing, in reality the distinctions between them are not always crystal clear. The relationship of SaaS to PaaS in particular can be complicated. A specific, complex Software-as-a-Service may use PaaS or even other more granular Software-as-a-Service. Even a PaaS may assemble lower-level pieces as a collection of software services. For example, most services will require an identity management (authentication, authorization, and accounting) service. This identity service is one of the key features a PaaS provides to applications. However, there is no reason that service cannot be, in turn, provided by some external SaaS! In this case, a key function of the PaaS is provided via a low-level SaaS.

Cloud Infrastructure Deployment Models

In addition to the functionality provided by a cloud, there are several different deployment models for clouds. *Public clouds* are the ones familiar to most developers. These cloud services are made available to the general public for a fee. The fee is generally on a usage basis, enabling organizations to utilize their operating budgets rather than their capital budgets. The customers have no need to maintain or operate the hardware or cloud infrastructure, leaving that responsibility completely to the cloud operator.

Amazon Web Services (AWS) is currently the largest public cloud and dominates the industry. Microsoft and VMware also operate public clouds, and a number of service providers do as well. Rackspace, in particular, provides an OpenStack-based public cloud, and is one of the primary contributors to the OpenStack project.

Private clouds, on the other hand, are internal to an organization. They represent the evolution of the traditional corporate data center. Only internal customers within the enterprise, and perhaps close partners, use private clouds. The corporate IT department or a contractor will purchase, setup, and maintain the hardware and software for the cloud. The cloud infrastructure may use charge-back to distribute costs among the business units, but the cloud itself is still dedicated to the single enterprise.

Organizations may operate private clouds for a number of reasons. The cost of a private cloud, if well run, may be less than utilizing the public clouds. Additionally, many industries have security or regulatory reasons that disallow the use of a public cloud for many workloads. These organizations are required to run those workloads in a private cloud. See Figure 1-2 for a look at the structure of public, private, and hybrid clouds.

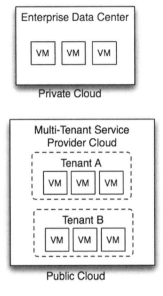

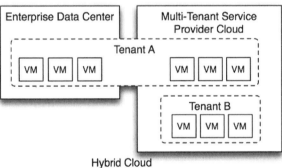

FIGURE 1-2

Hybrid clouds combine both private and public clouds. The goal with hybrid clouds is to keep general operating costs low by using the private cloud for most of the workloads, but to enable spillover into the public cloud when necessary. The spillover could happen due to capacity reasons—perhaps during the holiday season your private cloud doesn't have enough capacity—or for disaster recovery. This model avoids the capacity constraints of a private cloud while still keeping costs under control.

WHY SHOULD I CARE?

As an application developer or architect, you may wonder—why does all of this matter to me? All of this discussion covered so far focuses on the reason a business may want to move to the cloud. But why should that affect the application developer? The answer lies in a couple of different areas: the effect on the development process, and the effect on your application architecture.

Cloud services enable much more efficient processes for managing development, test, and production environments. These updated processes and methods represent the "DevOps" mentality—applying standard software development practices, such as source code version control, to the operational aspects of the application. This means capturing all of the configuration and deployment information in scripts and templates, and controlling their changes just as you would application code.

Scripts and templates can be built that produce a complete application environment. These can be used to automatically deploy not only the application, but also infrastructure required for the application, including virtual machines, networking, firewalls, load balancers, domain name services—you name it, and someone is working on making it available "as-a-Service." By automating the creation and destruction of these environments, you can ensure consistency between development, test, and production environments. For complex applications with many different services running on different machines, this can be a dramatic time saver.

OpenStack, and "as-a-Service" thinking in particular, will also end up changing the software and deployment architectures of your application. By relegating the common and routine functions to the cloud infrastructure, you free your time and thought to focus on the most important thing—your application's functionality. For example, a traditional application that allows large file uploads will need to designate temporary and permanent storage locations for those files, and manage the storage resources to ensure that the disk doesn't fill. The system administrator or deployer will need to devise a strategy to backup that data or replicate it to other data centers. But with the right cloud platform, you can simply delegate that function to the infrastructure, and get all of the benefits without devoting special effort.

Designing your application to work with the cloud services also dramatically simplifies scaling the application. The scalability of the individual services becomes the responsibility of the cloud operator, not the application developer or administrator. As long as the application makes effective use of those services, it will scale as needed with little to no work from the developers themselves.

Being able to utilize "as-a-Service" functions is one way your design will shift. Another is to plan for horizontal scaling rather than vertical scaling. That is, scaling by adding more machines (horizontally) rather than creating bigger machines (vertically). With most applications today, it is easiest to scale by getting a bigger, faster machine. This locks you into planning for peak capacity of each application individually. For each application you need to provision the largest machine you may need at peak load. But with applications built for the cloud, you instead scale by adding more machines. These machines can be smaller, and with cloud automation, can be added, removed, or resized as needed. This ability to scale up and down as needed is called *elastic scaling*, and is one of the key features of cloud computing.

A frequently used analogy is that traditional servers are like "pets," while cloud-based servers are "cattle." This describes a necessary shift in mentality for a traditional application architect. The idea is that a pet is unique and special, with its own unique name. A lot of resources are spent to raise and nurture one, and if it is sick, it will be nursed back to health. Cattle, on the other hand, are not treated specially or carefully raised. They are treated en masse—they are given numbers, not names—and a sick one is culled to prevent any spread of disease through the herd.

The implication here is that cloud-based servers should be disposable and easily re-deployed, and not require careful hand configuration. That way, if there is a problem with one, you do not spend time trying to figure it out and fix it—you simply replace it with a new one. This is the logical extension of the ability to scale elastically. Why take the time to figure out what's wrong with a machine when it's behaving badly? Just pull it out of the application and replace it with a new one while you debug the problem (not to fix that machine, but to prevent the issue in the future).

What Is OpenStack?

OpenStack bills itself as a "cloud operating system." Fundamentally, it solves the IaaS problem. It provides the ability to abstract the physical compute, storage, and networking resources into pools. Those resources can then be divvied up among users in a secure way. Users only need to pay for what they are using, rather than having to provision their applications for peak load.

OpenStack is a collection of open source software projects, backed by a non-profit organization, the OpenStack Foundation. These projects work together to provide a consistent API layer, while enabling the actual services to be provided by a variety of different vendor or open source implementations. At the core, these services include the functionality you need to run a cloud, that is, the ability to spin up virtual machines, the ability to allocate, manage, and share storage among those machines, and the ability enable these machines to communicate with one another securely over the network.

KEEPING TRACK OF RELEASES

OpenStack has official releases every six months. In order to make it easier to keep track of all these releases, they are given names in alphabetical order. Below is the name of each release, and its release date, through the Liberty release.

- ➤ Austin: October 2010
- ➤ Bexar: February 2011
- ➤ Cactus: April 2011
- ➤ Diablo: September 2011
- ➤ Essex: April 2012
- ➤ Folsom: September 2012
- ➤ Grizzly: April 2013
- ➤ Havana: October 2013
- ➤ Icehouse: April 2014
- ➤ Juno: October 2014
- ➤ Kilo: April 2015
- ➤ Liberty: October 2015

In addition to the release name, each release is identified by the year and release during that year—<year>.<release>.<patch>. For example, Kilo is also known as 2015.1, as the first release in 2015. Patch releases for Kilo are 2015.1.1, 2015.1.2, etc. The second major release of 2015 is Liberty, which is also known as 2015.2.

All of these services are accessible via RESTful APIs, as well as command-line interfaces and a web-based user interface called Horizon. Horizon is convenient for setting up things on an ad-hoc basis, but doesn't offer the full capabilities of the APIs—and of course the APIs and CLI tools can be easily scripted (see Figure 1-3).

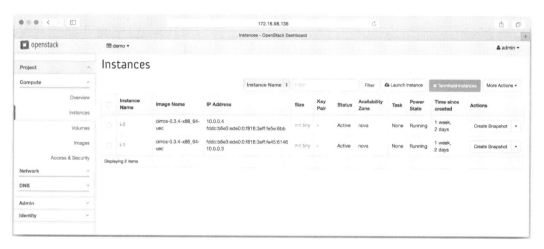

FIGURE 1-3

The next table shows the major services provided by OpenStack, along with their names. OpenStack community members will usually refer to each service by its name, so it's helpful to see them all in one place and get a handle on what each one does. In fact, there are many more services, but these are the most common ones you will find.

NAME	SERVICE	DESCRIPTION
Horizon	Dashboard	A graphical user interface for managing your cloud
Keystone	Identity	Authentication, authorization, and OpenStack service information
Nova	Compute	Spin up, manage, and terminate virtual machines
Cinder	Block Storage	Disk volumes (that outlive an instance) and snapshots of instances
Swift	Object Storage	Shared, replicated, redundant storage for images, files, and other media accessible via Hypertext Transfer Protocol (HTTP)
Neutron	Network	Provide secure tenant networking
Glance	Image	Provide storage and access to VM images and snapshots
Heat	Orchestration	Spin up groups of machines, networks, and other resources via templates

continues

(continued)

NAME	SERVICE	DESCRIPTION
Designate	DNS	Create domains and records in the DNS infrastructure
Ceilometer	Telemetry	Monitor resources usage across the cloud
Trove	Database	Provide access to private tenant databases
Ironic	Bare Metal	Spin up instances on physical hardware
Magnum	Containers	Manage containers within instances
Murano	Application	Deploy packaged applications across multiple instances
Sahara	Data Processing Cluster	Provides a Hadoop or Spark cluster as a service

A default installation of OpenStack will include "reference" versions of each service. For example, by default an OpenStack cloud will use the Kernel-based Virtual Machine (KVM) hypervisor to manage virtual machines. One of the most important aspects of the OpenStack architecture, however, is the driver or plugin-based nature of each service. With this design, you can use an implementation other than the reference one. In your cloud, you can swap out KVM with ESXi, Xen, or other hypervisors. The APIs used to launch and manage VMs remain the same, regardless of the underlying hypervisor. This same concept extends across OpenStack services, enabling the same APIs with different service implementations.

This level of flexibility behind the scenes, while providing a consistent API, is one of the keys to the success of OpenStack. Users can build their applications and automation on top of OpenStack, without having to worry that they are locking themselves into a single backend provider of computer, networking, or storage. The APIs won't change even if they swap out the backend.

OpenStack is frequently used in enterprises for private clouds, though there are some public cloud services that are based on it. There are also companies that will create and operate a private OpenStack cloud for you within their data centers. In this case, the hardware is not shared with other customers, so you have the predictability and security of the private cloud but do not have to find and hire the experts to maintain it.

Even in private cloud environments, OpenStack is a *multi-tenant* cloud platform. This means that multiple users or groups of users—*tenants*—can utilize the physical resources of the cloud, while keeping all of their virtualized resources private. For a tenant, the OpenStack environment appears, for the most part, to be theirs and theirs alone. But for the operator, the underlying physical resources and software systems are shared. In OpenStack, tenants are also sometimes referred to as *projects*.

In a multi-tenant OpenStack cloud, each tenant is allocated a *quota* for the various types of resources that may be used. The quota provides a maximum limit for that tenant for that particular resource. You will have a quota for CPUs, memory, storage, networks, subnets, and floating IPs, among other resources. This prevents any single tenant from consuming all of the resources.

Why OpenStack?

There are a number of cloud management platform options out there. The most obvious and dominant player is VMware with their vRealize suite of software. So, why should you take your time to learn about OpenStack rather than vRealize, AWS, Azure, CloudStack, or any of the other solutions?

About 15 years ago, IT professionals faced a very similar set of questions about Linux and proprietary UNIX systems. Solaris, HP-UX, AIX and their competitors were solid, well known, and widely deployed products, whereas Linux was a graduate student's project that was difficult to install and operate and was fairly immature, with driver and other compatibility issues. It was not clear at all at the time that spending effort learning and understanding Linux was worth it. History though, has proven that such a choice would have been the right one. All of those expensive, proprietary UNIX implementations have lost their value proposition—they really don't have much that is unique to offer anymore. Linux has continued to grow and has taken over most of the environments where those systems once thrived.

This isn't just a simple analogy. There is a relentless pressure in this industry to reduce costs, and to increase the velocity of feature delivery—deliver more, faster, and cheaper. The way to achieve "more, faster" is standardization. This is the same basic principle as building libraries and frameworks in programming. A standard architecture behaves in a predicable manner, providing core services on which you can rely and build. There is no need to repeat the process of developing that architecture over and over, allowing you to focus on the new functionality.

The way you achieve "cheaper" is to make those standards open and free. This combination of open and standard leads to *commoditization*—essentially the development of interchangeable components that are the same regardless of the manufacturer or vendor. Commodities imply a lot of competition, and there is little or no product differentiation for which to charge extra. This drives down the costs dramatically.

Linux has both of these characteristics—open and standard—in UNIX-like operating systems, and that is why it won. Not because it was better, but because it was cheaper and faster to use as a base for building new functionality. Linux is just one example, of course. This story has repeated over and over in the technology industry. With machine architectures we have the x86 platform, and standard architectures for memory, disks, and serial bus-based peripherals.

In fact, if you take the broader view, you can see that the commoditization has continuously moved up the value chain. It started with hardware, moved to operating systems, and these days even sophisticated databases and distributed system components are being commoditized. In databases, we used to have Informix, DB2, Oracle, Sybase, and others. But MySQL and PostgresSQL are open and standard, and they have completely dominated the low-end of the database market. Oracle still leads in the high-end, and is able to provide value in those more specialized environments, but as the open source products improve, the space for the proprietary vendors constricts.

In some way, cloud computing is the culmination of this commoditization process in the industry. Broadly, you can think of the revolution happening in the computing industry as a refocusing of the industry on the core functions of computing. The abstraction of the computing infrastructure into simply compute, storage, and networking components, and breaking of these out from being vertically integrated, to horizontally integrated, is truly transformative. It brings full commoditization to these elements, which are the basic foundation of the industry.

Cloud platform management will follow the same pattern. The proprietary platforms like vRealize will thrive for a time, but in the long run the open and standard systems will win. While there may always be a place for the proprietary solutions in more specialized environments, the most common platforms will be open source. You can see this already happening: the Zenoss 2014 State of the Open Source Cloud Survey (`http://www.zenoss.com/resource-center/white-papers`) found that 30 percent of respondents were already using an open source cloud, up 72 percent from 17.2 percent in 2012. Another 34 percent of the respondents planned to implement an open source cloud in the future. Understanding this gives you an advantage to focus on the eventual winner, instead of chasing what will ultimately be a setting star.

There are several open, standard cloud management platforms. So even if you believe that the bet on open and standard is the way to go, why should you bet on OpenStack? The answer here is simple—momentum. OpenStack is by far the most widely used and supported open source cloud management platform, and it has the largest community of developers and vendors push it forward. The same survey mentioned above found that 69 percent of respondents with an open source cloud were using OpenStack in 2014, up from 51 percent in 2012. An amazing 86 percent of those considering an open source cloud deployment are looking at OpenStack.

The OpenStack developer and user communities have grown dramatically as well. The OpenStack Foundation 2014 Annual Report (`https://www.openstack.org/assets/reports/osf-annual-report-2014.pdf`) provides detailed insight into this growth. In 2013, the best quarter for mean monthly active developers had 391 developers—in 2014 this measure was up 45 percent to 569 developers. Large investments from HP, Cisco, RedHat, IBM, Dell, Mirantis, Rackspace, and many other vendors have driven this surge. The incredible growth in the number of users, developers, and other interested parties can be seen from the attendance at the twice annual OpenStack Summits, seen in Figure 1-4 (source: openstack.org).

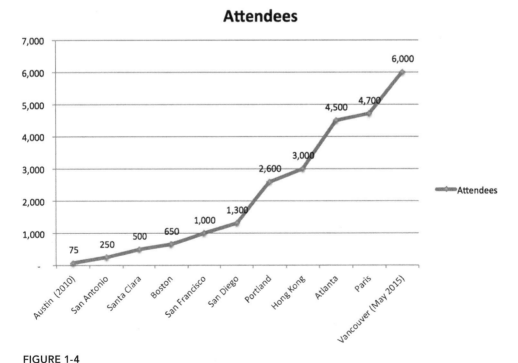

FIGURE 1-4

Clearly OpenStack has the momentum to succeed.

UNDERSTANDING THE ARCHITECTURE

OpenStack is built on a loosely coupled architecture. Each component is built independently and runs its own services. These services may be distributed among a number of different machines with different responsibilities. This enables scaling of particular functions, by adding machines with particular roles. It also enables redundancy; a highly available deployment will contain several of each type of machine.

Software Architecture

Individual components interact with one another via well-defined application programming interfaces (APIs)—typically based on representational state transfer (REST) conventions, though in some cases using remote procedure calls (RPC) or notifications over a message bus. Typically, these services will maintain data in a relational database—usually MySQL or PostgreSQL. The message bus and database are shared across services, but the interactions between those services remain clearly delineated. This enables different services to grow and change independently from the others, so long as they provide backward-compatibility in the APIs.

Each of the major services—compute (Nova), networking (Neutron), block storage (Cinder), etc.— have several internal processes and components. Generally, they will each have an API service that provides an HTTP-based RESTful API. This API service will communicate with the other components via the message bus.

The Horizon service is a web-based UI that interacts with the various services. Similarly, there are command-line tools to interact with each service. These tools are optional; you can build your own interface directly to the service APIs if you wish. Horizon and the official CLI clients do not have any special access; everyone uses the same APIs. Each client really only needs to be informed of the location of Keystone, the identity service. This service contains a catalog of all services and API endpoints available in the OpenStack platform (see Figure 1-5).

In Figure 1-5, what you see is a simplified depiction of how the services interact. Each service has an API component, which communicates with Keystone's API via HTTPS to provide authentication and authorization information. Each API service uses the message bus to communicate with several other processes for that service (just called "Services" in the diagram). As needed, these downstream service processes will call the APIs of other services. For example, Nova will call the Neutron API to acquire a port on a particular network.

Deployment Architecture

How are all of these different pieces of software deployed on the hardware? This is actually pretty flexible. For development or just experimentation, you can even run everything on a single machine. However, a more typical deployment will have several controller nodes (for high availability purposes), along with additional network, compute, and controller nodes.

Each high-level service (compute, networking, storage, and others) consists of multiple daemons (background processes). These daemons are spread out across the various types of nodes. That is, you do not run individual services on individual nodes, but rather spread each service out across different types of nodes.

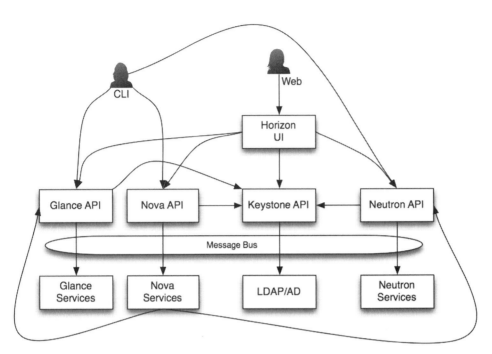

FIGURE 1-5

For example, all of the services share the database and messaging components (typically MySQL and RabbitMQ, respectively). You may run these each on separate clusters, with each cluster spread over different failure domains. Additionally, you may have several physical nodes that provide the API endpoints, behind a physical load balancer. Different daemons for Nova and Neutron will be spread across the network and compute nodes. Figure 1-6 shows a simplified diagram of this layout.

Notice the different types of nodes in Figure 1-6. *Compute nodes* run the hypervisor and therefore the actual VM instances, as well as provide the ephemeral storage for instances. They will also run Neutron networking agents to manage the connectivity between VMs (called *east-west traffic*).

The *network nodes* usually provide the connectivity between VMs and outside the cloud (called *north-south traffic*), as well as the advanced network services like load balancing and VPN access. Depending on the choices made by the administrators and users, there may be agents providing network routing services on the network nodes, directly on the compute nodes, or both.

The *block storage nodes* provide volume services to the instances—that is, they provide access to persistent storage for disk volumes that can be attached and detached to instances. Clouds that offer *object storage* will also have separate clusters for that. Object storage provides shared, replicated, redundant storage for images, files, and other media accessible via HTTP.

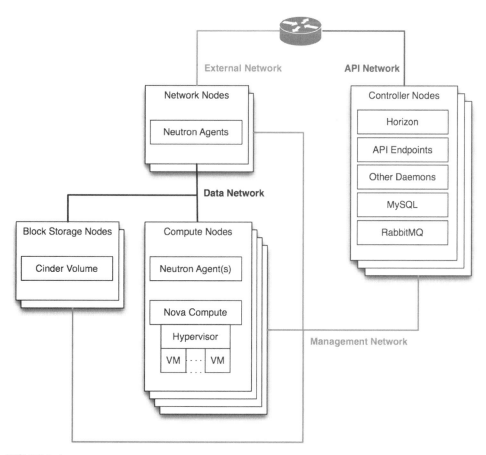

FIGURE 1-6

Various segregated networks connect all of these nodes. Every node is accessible via the *management network*, which is used for different parts of OpenStack to communicate with one another. All of the message bus, database, and cross-project API traffic go over the management network. The *data network* connects all of the compute nodes, network nodes, and block storage nodes. The internal cloud tenant traffic is carried on this network, whereas the *external network* provides access to the outside world. Since the compute nodes do not communicate with the outside world, but only with other nodes in the cloud infrastructure, they need not have connectivity to the external network, but only need access to the data network. Only the network nodes need to connect to the external network. Finally, some installations will use an *API network*, which provides access between the outside world and the OpenStack end points (API and Horizon), separate from the external network used by tenants.

Pros and Cons

This architecture provides a great deal of flexibility. This enables the scalability by letting the cloud operator deploy additional nodes to scale the infrastructure. It also allows the ability to create highly available services, since you can split each service out and make them redundant across failure domains. However, it is very complex, and can be quite difficult to set up and maintain.

As a user of the cloud, this will be transparent to you. But a properly run cloud will have enough redundancy built in that you can expect a high-level of reliability from the OpenStack infrastructure.

Another substantial benefit to this architecture is avoiding vendor lock-in. Each service provides a plugin or driver-based architecture. This enables each service to work with any number of vendor platforms to provide the actual service. For compute, you can use the default KVM hypervisor, ESXi, Xen, or one of many other hypervisor choices. The networking service defaults to using Open vSwitch to provide Layer 2 (the data link or MAC address layer) connectivity, and the Linux networking stack (iptables, routing, and namespaces) to implement Layer 3 (IP layer) functionality. However, there are more than 20 different vendor plugins to swap all or part of that default implementation. In fact, these vendor implementations can be used at the same time, in the same cloud.

By avoiding vendor lock-in, OpenStack enables more competition between the vendors, pushing down prices in the market. The ability to use multiple vendors at once makes transitioning from one vendor to another more feasible, and also allows the choice of vendor for solving specific use cases.

An interesting feature introduced with the Kilo release of OpenStack is federated identity. This takes the distributed nature of OpenStack and allows it to span across multiple clouds, even from different providers. Two cloud providers can set up a trust relationship, enabling users of one provider to use the same credentials with another, trusted provider. Thus the same workload management tools you use for a single cloud can theoretically be used to manage workloads across multiple clouds. For capacity burst use cases, this is a powerful feature.

OpenStack Distributions

With the complexity of the architecture, a number of companies have stepped in to help with installation and management of an OpenStack platform in a private cloud. These include names familiar from the Linux distribution world, such as RedHat, SUSE, and Canonical (Ubuntu), as well as new players that are focused only on OpenStack, such as Mirantis.

INDUSTRY CONSOLIDATION

In fact the OpenStack industry has seen a great deal of consolidation in 2014 and 2015. Several pure-play OpenStack companies have been gobbled up by the bigger players.

Many large integrators and enterprise software vendors are also jumping into the OpenStack distribution game, with the likes of IBM, HP, and Oracle joining the fray.

If you don't have an OpenStack cloud available already, or you want to learn more about the architecture and how all of the pieces fit together, you can setup your own OpenStack playground. You can use one of these distributions to setup your own small cloud. Each of the distribution vendors provides their own tools for setup of OpenStack. They are primarily targeted at production environments, and as such can be pretty hard to get started with on your own. For example, Canonical's offering requires a minimum of seven physical nodes just to bring up the environment.

If you are setting something up small, your best options are probably RedHat's open source distribution (as opposed to their supported version running on RedHat Enterprise Linux), called RDO (www.rdoproject.org). The nice thing about this distribution is that it offers a simple "all in one" option to deploy the entire environment on a single node.

If you would like to tinker with the actual code of the various OpenStack services, you could also setup a *devstack* environment. Devstack (www.devstack.org) is a powerful set of scripts to create and configure an OpenStack development environment.

While the detailed instructions online are quite good, here are a few hints to make your devstack setup go smoothly. You'll want a fresh Ubuntu (http://www.ubuntu.com) or Fedora (www.fedoraproject.org) installation. Don't try to run devstack on your regular machine—you'll want a dedicated machine (virtual or physical). If you have a virtualization product like VMware Workstation or Fusion, or the free VirtualBox for your laptop or desktop, the best thing to do is create a base server installation of your OS of choice (enabling all of the extra repositories), and then snapshot it. This will make it easy to start over if you trash your environment.

The instructions will have you create a local.conf file, which the devstack scripts use to capture all of the specifics of your installation. There are only a few items you need to set in your local.conf.

```
[[local|localrc]]
ADMIN_PASSWORD=stack
DATABASE_PASSWORD=$ADMIN_PASSWORD
RABBIT_PASSWORD=$ADMIN_PASSWORD
SERVICE_PASSWORD=$ADMIN_PASSWORD
SERVICE_TOKEN=some-random-string
FIXED_RANGE=10.0.0.0/24
FLOATING_RANGE=192.168.20.0/25
PUBLIC_NETWORK_GATEWAY=192.168.20.1

LOGFILE=/opt/stack/logs/stack.log

disable_service n-net
enable_service neutron q-svc q-agt q-dhcp q-l3 q-meta
```

The first section here sets up the networking. You should pick a FIXED_RANGE that does not overlap your existing network. Your FLOATING_RANGE can correspond to an existing unused subnet on your network, with the PUBLIC_NETWORK_GATEWAY being the local default gateway on your subnet.

The LOGFILE setting simply helps you debug if your devstack does not come up properly, whereas the remainder of the file disables Nova networking and enables Neutron networking.

You will need access to either devstack or another OpenStack instance to follow the examples throughout this book.

GETTING THE OPENSTACK CLI CLIENTS

To follow along with the examples, you'll need access to a machine with the OpenStack clients installed. You can learn how to install the clients at `http://docs.openstack.org/cli-reference/content/`, which will include instructions for a variety of operating systems. The examples in this book will use Linux.

The easiest way to use these clients is to set the necessary authentication information in environment variables:

```
$ export OS_USERNAME=username OS_PASSWORD=password ↵
  OS_TENANT_NAME=tenant-name
$ export OS_AUTH_URL=http://keystone-ip:keystone-port/v2.0
```

This allows you to call the clients without passing those parameters:

```
$ openstack flavor list
+----+-----------+-------+------+-----------+-------+-----------+
| ID | Name      |   RAM | Disk | Ephemeral | VCPUs | Is Public |
+----+-----------+-------+------+-----------+-------+-----------+
| 1  | m1.tiny   |   512 |    1 |         0 |     1 | True      |
| 2  | m1.small  |  2048 |   20 |         0 |     1 | True      |
| 3  | m1.medium |  4096 |   40 |         0 |     2 | True      |
| 4  | m1.large  |  8192 |   80 |         0 |     4 | True      |
| 42 | m1.nano   |    64 |    0 |         0 |     1 | True      |
| 5  | m1.xlarge | 16384 |  160 |         0 |     8 | True      |
| 84 | m1.micro  |   128 |    0 |         0 |     1 | True      |
+----+-----------+-------+------+-----------+-------+-----------+
```

If your services endpoints are using HTTPS, you'll need to change the `OS_AUTH_URL` to reflect that. If you are using self-signed certificates, you also need to pass in the `-insecure` option.

SUMMARY

In this chapter, you have learned about the various types of cloud computing—IaaS, PaaS, and SaaS—and how they related to one another. OpenStack fills the IaaS, and perhaps in the future the PaaS functions, in the clouds. More importantly you learned that driving costs lower while delivering more features, more quickly is the driving force behind the cloud computing revolution. Finally, you learned about the major components of OpenStack—Nova, Neutron, Glance, and Keystone, and how to set up a playground for experimenting with OpenStack.

Understanding the OpenStack Ecosystem: Core Projects

WHAT'S IN THIS CHAPTER?

➤ How the different OpenStack components work together and how authentication works within the infrastructure

➤ A look at how a compute instance is composed and the different hypervisors supported in OpenStack

➤ How data is stored in the infrastructure and understanding the differences between Block Storage and Object Storage

➤ How instance templates and snapshots are created and where they are stored

➤ The different ways to manage your OpenStack resources: GUI versus CLI versus APIs

➤ How the network is designed in OpenStack and the different network components available and exposed through the APIs

At this point, you have an understanding of why cloud computing is important to application developers, and a general overview of OpenStack. In this chapter, you will learn the core services in more detail. These are the services most critical to running an application—compute, network, and storage. You will also learn about the management services to make those possible, such as the identity service, which allows you to authenticate in order to create your applications.

Sometimes, it may seem that the descriptions in this chapter go into more detail than you need to run an application. However, you can think of these features as tools and building blocks. You need to have a solid understanding of what is *possible*, so you can see new ways to build flexible, scalable, and robust applications (see Figure 2-1).

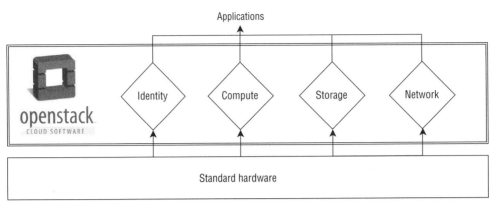

FIGURE 2-1

IDENTITY

The identity service within OpenStack, named Keystone, is responsible for authentication, authorization and accounting (AAA) and currently implements and provides the OpenStack Identity API.

The main goal of this identity service is to process and validate authentication and authorization requests, then return an "authentication token," which is used to authenticate the user against the APIs and can be used to contact the other services of an OpenStack infrastructure. These services can be discovered using the catalog returned in the authentication response (detailed later in this chapter).

Keystone currently implements two versions of the Identity API (v2, v3). The second version has been used for years and is still mainly used today in the different libraries and clients supporting OpenStack. The third version is quite recent and provides a more pluggable and flexible design, allowing using multiple authentication mechanisms (the original "password" method, but moreover well-known and used mechanisms, such as OAuth or SAML2), and the ability to combine these methods in a single request.

This last Identity API has a multi-tenant design and has simple resources:

➤ **Region**: an OpenStack infrastructure that optionally may have sub-regions

➤ **Service with Endpoints**: an OpenStack registered service in Keystone that can have zero, one, or multiple endpoints to reach this one (e.g. public, internal, admin)

➤ **Domain**: a container for the users, groups, and projects

➤ **Project** (known as "*Tenant*" in the second version of the API): owning a set of OpenStack resources

➤ **User**: a single API consumer, which should have really restricted authorizations in your application

➤ **Group**: a collection of different users of the same domain

➤ **Role**: an authorization that a user or a group of users can obtain on a project or a domain

All of these resources can be managed using the Identity Admin API, which is available as a create, read, update, and delete (CRUD) RESTful API.

Using Tokens and Re-Authentication

The authentication against the different OpenStack services is based on tokens provided by the identity service (Keystone) or configured in the service itself (e.g. admin tokens).

A token provided by an identity service is an arbitrary string that contains the *User* identity and optionally an authorization called *scope*. The authorization attached to this token grants access to a *Project* or a *Domain*, allowing you to access *Project* or *Domain*-related resources.

You can easily create a token using the Identity API with the method POST /auth/tokens with a user identity and the wanted scope:

```
{
    "auth": {
        "identity": { ... },
        "scope": { ... }
    }
}
```

Token Identities

When requesting a new token, the identity parameter will contain the used authentication mechanisms. Here is an example using password. The unique identifier of the user is used here, however it is possible to use the username if the domain is explicitly specified.

```
{
    "auth": {
        "identity": {
            "methods": [
                "password"
            ],
            "password": {
                "user": {
                    "id": "042042",
                    "password": "secret-password"
                }
            }
        }
    }
}
```

Scoped and Non-Scoped Tokens

If specified in the request, the authorization scope must contain the project identifier or the domain identifier.

```
{
    "auth": {
        "scope": {
            "project": {
```

```
                        "id": "123456"
                    }
                }
            }
        }
```

If a scope has been provided in the token creation request, the Identity API will return a `catalog` containing the different OpenStack services that can be used by the user with the token and the `roles` granted to this user.

```
    X-Subject-Token: ff00ff84
    {
        "token": {
            "catalog": [
                {
                    "endpoints": [
                        {
                            "id": "c3ac301342a381b895743659d0956de1",
                            "interface": "public",
                            "region": "RegionOne",
                            "url": "http://my.identity.service:5000"
                        }
                    ],
                    "id": " 9192d6fb0f120a188133cb569b8db832",
                    "type": "identity",
                    "name": "keystone"
                }
            ],
            "expires_at": "2015-07-14T13:37:00.000000Z",
            "issued_at": "2015-07-15T13:37:00.000000Z",
            "methods": [
                "password"
            ],
            "user": {
                "id": "042042"
            }
        }
    }
```

If no `scope` is specified in the token creation request, the Identity API will return a non-scoped token that can be used to identify the user in a next Identity API request. One example would be to create a scoped token using the `token` authentication mechanism.

A scoped token can be re-scoped using the `token` authentication mechanism with a smaller scope, for example this is extremely useful to provide a limited authorized token to an application sub-component or another API client that doesn't need the full authorization of the original token to operate.

Using an Authentication Token

The obtained authentication tokens can be passed in all of the HTTP requests against the different REST APIs as a `X-Auth-Token` HTTP header. These tokens will be checked by the requested OpenStack service to ensure their validity (i.e. expiration, revocation, etc.) and if the authorization of this token allows access to the requested resource with the policy of the service applied to the user role.

How Various Pieces of OpenStack Communicate with Each Other

OpenStack has a modular architecture where all of the different components are separate services that communicate together using standardized REST APIs (see Figure 2-2). This principle is fundamental and required in the OpenStack project life because different teams led by different people are developing each component. All of the OpenStack components' features and updates start by an API design discussion. All of these APIs should be simple, standard, re-usable and re-implementable by any developer who would want to use them and have custom services that would implement the API open-specifications. Moreover, these standard REST APIs have features that use a messaging queue to internally process the different actions and events.

The requests processed between the different OpenStack services are authenticated with the tokens of the original request (see the earlier section about authentication token generation) and the authorization of these requests between the OpenStack services are checked as a direct request to the end-service.

For example, when a user creates a snapshot of a compute instance, the compute service processes a request against the image service to store this snapshot. When creating this request, the original authentication token is passed in the REST API request between the two services. If this image service uses the object storage service as a storage backend, an authenticated request is generated between these two services using the original authentication token (see Figure 2-2).

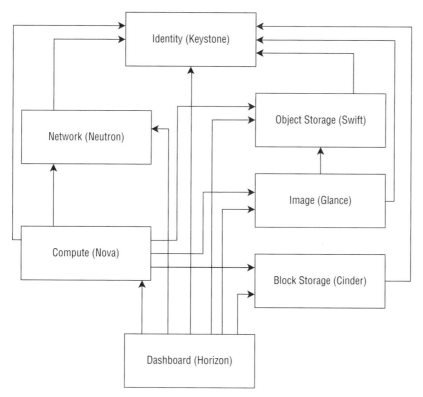

FIGURE 2-2

Can Applications Use Keystone?

When creating an application that uses OpenStack, the usage of Keystone is required to ensure appropriate authorizations and structure of the different services or parts of the application.

Let's take the example of an application that would have documents (e.g. pictures) uploaded by a guest user. So, we need a service to convert or resize these pictures. We also need to store the pictures (that we call objects) using an OpenStack object storage service. We then need to automatically provision and manage the instances using the compute instances. We'll have two different roles or projects and two different users because we don't want the public accessible application to manage our instances for security reasons.

> **DEMO APPLICATION SOURCE CODE**
>
> You can access the source code from our demo application via GitHub: `https://github.com/johnbelamaric/openstack-appdev-book`.

COMPUTE

The Compute project in OpenStack, named Nova, includes all of the APIs and tools to provision and manage the instances (the virtual machines provisioned on physical compute nodes) across multiple physical hosts at scale. This project provides an abstraction of the configuration of the main used hypervisors in the world, allowing you to easily provision virtual machines with a standard API, independent of a specific hypervisor technology.

In this part, you'll discover the different pieces that compose an instance on OpenStack, how the instances models are managed (called *flavors*), how the instances are scheduled in a compute infrastructure and the main hypervisors supported by the project (See Figure 2-3).

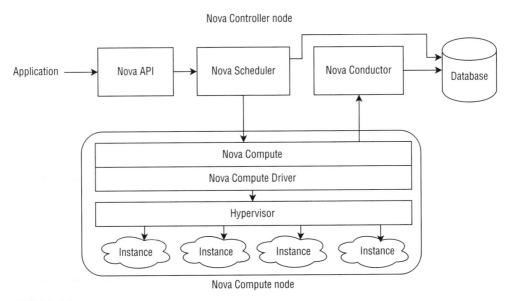

FIGURE 2-3

Pieces of an Instance

In OpenStack, an instance has the traditional components of a virtualized server provided by a hypervisor. These characteristics are defined by the flavors in the compute service:

➤ One or multiple allocated dedicated or virtual CPUs (*vCPUs*)

➤ Some allocated memory (RAM)

➤ A root disk that can be any device attached to the host server (virtual or not virtual, local, remote, or distributed)

The instances have usually one or multiple networks configured. These networks can be configured using the network service (Neutron), and the network devices can be provisioned by the Nova service in the host using the Network API and configured in the instance by the hypervisor.

The instances can have persistent block storages attached to them (i.e. a virtual hard drive in the instance), which can be provisioned and managed using the volume service and attached by the hypervisor to the instance.

The console (screen) of an instance can be viewed using the VNC service in Nova, which can be compared to a physical keyboard, video and mouse (KVM) for a physical server. KVM was traditionally used to share these devices with multiple computers (https://en.wikipedia.org/wiki/KVM_switch). Today the same term is used to describe the virtual access to these input/outputs of an OpenStack instance. This Nova service is presented as a good way to abstract the way to access all of the graphical interfaces and consoles of all the instances, regardless of the used virtualization technology and the instances' operative systems. There are different protocols to access an instance's interface and Nova provides a unified and transparent way to access them. For example, this service can also proxy a RDP (Remote Desktop Protocol) for the instances that run Microsoft Windows.

Understanding Flavors

A *flavor* in OpenStack represents a model of an instance: a set of allocated resources for a virtual machine and its specificities. In public cloud services where host servers are shared across multiple projects or tenants (customers), the flavors can be compared to commercial offers, where the billed resources are calculated using the total time the instances of a specific flavor run during a month. This information is calculated using the OpenStack Telemetry Service (Ceilometer, see section 3.6).

A compute flavor contains some of the following resource details:

➤ The name of a unique identifier

➤ The amount of cores (vCPUs) and the weight if they are shared with multiple instances

➤ The memory (RAM) and the swap size

➤ The root disk and ephemeral disk space

A flavor may contain extra specifications that are useful to make decisions during the scheduling of an instance in a compute infrastructure, and to allocate the required resource to run the instance (e.g. processor architecture, over-provisioning, PCI devices required etc.). The flavors may be public or linked to some specific OpenStack projects. Since we can associate this to a commercial offer or a compute instance model, a specific model (or compute instance) can be limited to a simple project or can be public and used by any project in an OpenStack infrastructure. For example, when you launch a new processor model for customers in a public cloud, you could create dedicated flavors to allow them to use these new physical server models to create new instances.

Scheduling Filters

When an instance is provisioned on an OpenStack compute infrastructure, one task of Nova, and especially of its scheduler, is to choose the compute node (physical host) where the instance will be created or moved. You can find an overview of the scheduler operations (Filtering and Weighting) in Figure 2-4.

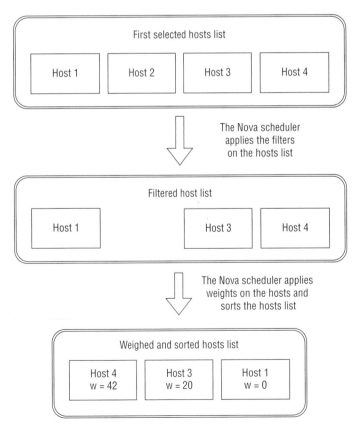

FIGURE 2-4

Filtering

This task is processed using a simple concept: the compute scheduler takes a set of nodes available to use and applies a set of filters to this list to eliminate the ones that don't match the different criteria of the required configuration (refer to Figure 2-4).

Here are some examples of scheduling filters:

➤ Skip the hosts that are full (no CPU, Memory or disk available)

➤ Match only a host that has the exact amount of resources available

➤ Use the same host of another instance

➤ Use a physical host where some specific PCI devices are available

The physical hosts can be added in aggregation groups that are usually used to match one or multiple specific flavors or projects using a scheduling filter. Here are two common use cases of this feature:

➤ An aggregation group can be created for a customer with some dedicated hosts and hardware. Using extra specifications in a dedicated flavor (private for a domain, a project, or multiple projects), when the user will create an instance using this specific flavor the scheduler will filter only the hosts contained in this specific aggregation group.

➤ Some hosts with specific hardware (e.g. SSD hard drives, specific CPU architecture, etc.) or allocation rules (e.g. dedicated resources, over-provisioned resources) can be set in an aggregation group and the matching flavors created. Here the hosts may be shared with all of the projects (customers) of the compute infrastructure and the flavor will act as a public commercial offer where the hosts are shared with some specifies.

Weights

Once the hosts are filtered, the scheduler applies some weights on each resource of the host or instance to determine the best host to choose to allocate and install the instance. For example, we could add a higher weight to fill an almost full physical server with an instance that exactly matches the remaining amount of reserved and allocable resources, or conversely to set higher weight to the less-used servers and get the one that is currently the less loaded.

Types of Hypervisors

The companies or contributors of hypervisor products or projects are usually the main contributor of compute virtualization drivers. It is easy to add a custom driver that implements one part or all of the features abstracted by the compute service, which is available via the compute API.

Libvirt

The *libvirt* in Linux is an abstraction library to access and manage the virtual machines and containers in a Linux server and their network and storage configuration. It supports multiple technologies: KVM/QEMU, Xen, VirtualBox, VMware ESX, Hyper-V, OpenVZ, LXC, etc.

This is the default driver used by OpenStack and the most popular one for the kernel-based virtual machine/quick emulator (KVM/QEMU) virtualization. One of the pro arguments is managing the virtual machines regardless of the virtualization technology. But using the libvirt and its OpenStack driver has some weaknesses, especially given how it is mainly designed for KVM/QEMU, and some features provided by other virtualization technologies might be hidden by this abstraction layer. Hopefully other virtualization technologies are directly supported using their own Nova drivers.

VMware

Using VMware in OpenStack allows you to enjoy the advantages of both technologies: virtualization features for VMware and management/standard APIs for OpenStack.

VMware provides a great virtualization technology that provides the following:

➤ High Availability (HA); the ability to automatically reboot an instance on a full working hardware when an issue is detected by the hypervisor. In the marketed world of VMware, the "HA" is more branded as "fault tolerance."

➤ Fault tolerance (the live migration without restart of an instance on a working host when a host is down).

➤ Distributed Resource Scheduler (DRS), the smart dispatching of the running instances depending of the resources usage in real time.

For storage you can directly use the VMware datastore technology in Cinder and Glance, allowing you to manage all of your blocks using the standard block storage APIs.

STORAGE

The concept of object storage (named *Swift* in OpenStack) can be quite complicated to understand for an application developer when you are using a local file system to store all of the static medias (e.g. images, videos, music, etc.) and documents created and used by your application. But this is often one of the main steps to horizontally scale an application that uses these medias.

Good examples are the traditional content management systems (CMS) and blog engines that by default store locally all of the medias uploaded using the web application. This transition to an object storage infrastructure for any application is not always easy to realize since the code often needs to be partially rewritten to support this new storage system. It needs to be re-written because an application needs to change the way it accesses files (objects), for instance accessing local files in a hard drive is not the same as accessing objects using a REST API.

There are advantages for switching to object storage:

➤ You don't have to worry about the total space size; this is the job of the infrastructure provider, and an object storage service like Swift easily scales horizontally.

➤ You can split objects into multiple small blocks and the size of an object can almost be unlimited.

➤ You can store an unlimited number of objects in a single *container* or *bucket* of objects.

➤ The replication of the objects is done at the infrastructure level; it can even be done across multiple infrastructure regions.

Here are some potential blocking design and implementation points when you want to switch an application using a local file system to an object storage service:

➤ You can access your objects only using HTTP(s), but this can be great when the clients of your application are already using the HTTP protocol: you can provide access to an object without having to download it in your application server.

➤ Object storage is not a file system and should not be used like one. One of the worst examples is to try to match an existing file system hierarchy when developing an application using an application. In many use cases, the hierarchy logic should be on the application-side and the object storage should only contain the object data (blobs). The best example of this bad usage is renaming (moving) objects in OpenStack Swift. Since the dispatching of the objects across the storage infrastructure is based on a hash of the object name, the object will be copied between two servers and deleted from the source server. Moreover renaming a virtual directory (in fact an object with a mime-type specific to a directory) means renaming each object of the directory.

Introducing OpenStack Swift

The Swift service (OpenStack's object storage) provides all of the OpenStack projects with a HTTP REST API, allowing the processing of all the common operations on a stored object using the standard HTTP design and features to manage the resources (see Figure 2-5).

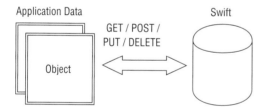

FIGURE 2-5

This project is horizontally scalable, distributed and highly available by design with different main components:

➤ **Swift proxy server:** this service dispatches the HTTP requests accessing the different objects to all the backend nodes. This component can be easily scaled since the positions of an object in an infrastructure are determined by hashing its name and finding its position using a ring algorithm.

➤ **Swift account server:** this service is responsible for storing the listing of the containers in the different existing accounts.

➤ **Swift container server:** this is similar to the account server, but responsible for listing the objects in a container.

➤ **Swift object server:** this is a storage backend installable on a physical host that provides an internal object storage API to manage the objects stored on the local server.

All of these components must be replicated and can be horizontally replicated to infinity (see Figure 2-6).

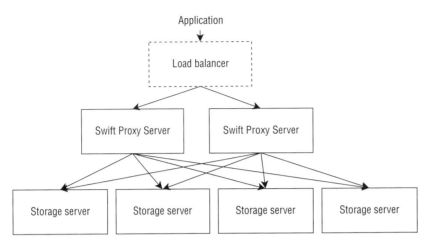

FIGURE 2-6

Eventual Consistency

OpenStack Swift is eventually consistent. For example, if a container server is under a heavy load and an object is PUT, the object will be available to GET as soon as the object is stored in different object servers, and as soon as the Swift proxy server handling the HTTP request responds to the client with success. In other words, the proxy stores the object in several objects' servers, and then responds to the PUT with a successful HTTP response. However, the addition of the object in the listing by the container server may be queued and delayed, and a GET request on the container may not list this new object. Another example is that by deleting an object (DELETE), an empty object is created with a more recent modification timestamp to ensure that the file can't be synchronized again if object server replica, where the object is stored, is down. Depending upon the synchronization delay between the different object servers storing the object, this might be available for a moment after the DELETE operation.

Storing Your First Object In Swift

The first step to store an object in your Swift account is to create a container for it. Containers regroup multiple objects with the same purpose using a specific set of settings. The grant to publicly read it or list it is an example. You can easily create it using the API with `curl` as the HTTP client:

```
$ curl -I -X PUT $swift/my-container -H "X-Auth-Token: $token"
HTTP/1.1 202 Accepted
Content-Length: 76
Content-Type: text/html; charset=UTF-8
X-Trans-Id: 5B44C388:EB0D_05C4F7D0:01BB_55AEDF79_18A38C8:4451
Date: Mon, 27 Jul 2015 22:25:40 GMT
Connection: close
```

As mentioned earlier, the authentication is done using a token created using the identity service and specified as a `X-Auth-Token` HTTP header.

Once the container is created, it is now possible to store the objects inside of it. To realize this action, another PUT request can be processed against the new stored resource path:

```
$ curl -I -X PUT -T $object $swift/my-container/my-object
HTTP/1.1 201 Created
Last-Modified: Mon, 27 Jul 2015 22:25:43 GMT
Content-Length: 0
Etag: 168e1afe97b471eb8948a1b612283d04
Content-Type: text/html; charset=UTF-8
X-Trans-Id: 5B44C388:35C8_05C4F7D0:01BB_55B6AFE5_2125569:444C
Date: Mon, 27 Jul 2015 22:25:42 GMT
Connection: close
```

That's all! Your first object is stored in your OpenStack object storage service and is now privately accessible using the HTTP API:

```
$ curl -X GET -i $swift/my-container/my-object.json \
    -H "X-Auth-Token: $ktoken"
HTTP/1.1 200 OK
Content-Length: 42
Accept-Ranges: bytes
Last-Modified: Mon, 27 Jul 2015 22:25:43 GMT
Etag: 168e1afe97b471eb8948a1b612283d04
X-Timestamp: 1438035942-04822
Content-Type: application/json
X-Trans-Id: 5B44C388:CCFA_05C4F7C0:01BB_55B6B352_1039A1B:637A
Date: Mon, 27 Jul 2015 22:40:18 GMT
Connection: close

[...]
```

All of these requests can be executed using the command line from the *Python Swift Client* (https://github.com/openstack/python-swiftclient). This provides a simple way to browse your accounts, containers, and objects:

```
# Upload an object
$ swift upload <container> <file_or_directory>

# Download an object
$ swift download <container> <object>
```

Temporary Swift URLs

Any request processed against the OpenStack Swift API can be pre-authenticated with a cryptographic signature. This mechanism allows the sharing of an authorization to access a single resource with a single HTTP method (e.g. POST swift/my-container/my-object) that can be used by third-party software, or a browser. This mechanism is really convenient if your application is multi-tenant and shares a single Swift Account for multiple users.

Let's take the example of an application that will store some PDF bills in an object container and will return to a customer of this application a temporary link to download one of them. The application will be able to return to the browser a signed URL to only GET the object for a limited time.

The signature will be verified using a secret key set in your account.

```
# Set the key as a account metadata "X-Account-Meta-Temp-Url-Key"
$ swift post -m "Temp-URL-Key:92cfceb39d57d914ed8b14d0e37643de0797ae56"


# Display the account information (returned as HTTP headers when
# processing a 'GET /v1/AUTH_account' request)
$ swift stat
Account: AUTH_account
Containers: 1
Objects: 42
Bytes: 4200
Meta Temp-Url-Key: 92cfceb39d57d914ed8b14d0e37643de0797ae56
Connection: close
X-Timestamp: 1365615113.11739
X-Trans-Id: 5B44C388:D669_5CDEF184:01BB_55C72581_2160:50A3
Content-Type: text/plain; charset=utf-8
Accept-Ranges: bytes
```

Here is an example of a temporary URL that contains two additional query strings: the timestamp representing the link expiration date (temp_url_expires) and the cryptographic signature itself (temp_url_sign):

```
/v1/AUTH_acount/c/o?temp_url_sig=9da40a8a7e288027809129d03ea2e5b09be70↵
d57&temp_url_expires=1439116248
```

For testing purposes and when using a terminal, you can easily create temporary links by using the swift-temp-url (https://github.com/openstack/swift/blob/master/bin/swift-temp-url) tool from the OpenStack Swift project. Here, though, is a programmatic example in Python that could be used in your application:

```
#! /usr/bin/env python

import hmac
from hashlib import sha1
from time import time

# Expiration timestamp for the link, here this one is in 1h
expires = int(time() + 60 * 60)
# Method authorized by the signed URL
method = 'GET'
# Relative path of the object from the server origin
path = '/v1/AUTH_account/c/o'
# The 'X-Account-Meta-Temp-URL-Key' meta of your Swift account
key = '92cfceb39d57d914ed8b14d0e37643de0797ae56'

# Signature calculation
hmac_body = '%s\n%s\n%s' % (method, expires, path)
signature = hmac.new(key, hmac_body, sha1).hexdigest()

# Format temporary URL
u = 'https://{host}/{path}?temp_url_sig={sig}&temp_url_expires={expires}'
url = u.format(
```

```
            host='swift.example.com', path=path,
            sig=signature, expires=expires
    )
```

Public Containers and Access Control List (ACLs)

If your application will only store public documents in a container, you can mark this one as public by using OpenStack Swift ACLs.

In a similar fashion the *temporary URL key* can be stored as an account metadata. These ACLs are stored at the container level as container metadata X-Container-Read to allow public access or listing of the container, or at the account level X-Account-Access-Control to allow other accounts of the infrastructure to access to the account.

Let's focus on the container-level ACLs. They have the following format: [item[,item…]] and thus can be combined. Two concepts are usable: the referral to grant (.referrer:example.com, or .r:example.com to reduce the length of the list) and the ability to list the container object (.rlistings).

Here is how you can allow anyone to access your public documents in your container and list them.

```
    # Set the new ACL
    $ swift post -r '.r:*,.rlistings' os-book

    # List the container "os-book" metadatas
    $ swift stat os-book
    Account: AUTH_account
    Container: os-book
    Objects: 42
    Bytes: 0
    Read ACL: .r:*,.rlistings
    Write ACL:
    Sync To:
    Sync Key:
    Accept-Ranges: bytes
    X-Trans-Id: 5B44C388:D847_5CDEF18E:01BB_55C72C0D_155E:1586
    X-Storage-Policy: Policy-0
    Connection: close
    X-Timestamp: 1439116292-30845
    Content-Type: text/plain; charset=utf-8
```

Understanding Block Storage

Sometimes when you use an OpenStack compute instance, you may need additional storage that can be mounted as volume in the instance. This type of storage is called "block" or "block storage."

Each block acts and is available in a single instance as an individual volume. A block is provisioned by the OpenStack block storage service (Cinder), which provides a target to access and mount the volume in the host and make it accessible in an instance.

Multiple storage backend drivers are available that allow you to have almost any storage infrastructure behind a standard abstraction layer. Here are the main storage backend technologies that can be used with Cinder.

Ceph

Ceph is a distributed a scalable storage solution that replicates its data across multiple storage servers. Ceph can be used as object storage (RADOS), block storage (RBD, RADOS block device), and a shared file system (Ceph FS). Ceph block devices (RBD) are resizable, thin-provisioned, store the data in RADOS, and are striped across multiple storage daemons (OSD).

Gluster

Gluster is a distributed and shared file system that can be used both as a block storage backend and object storage backend. In OpenStack, Gluster is exposed in a similar way as network file storage (NFS).

ZFS

ZFS (or Zettabyte File System) is a huge evolution compared to all of the existing file systems. As its name suggests, this one supports an almost unlimited storage size and simplifies the administration and the security of the files systems.

To achieve this goal, an extra abstraction level exists between the hard drives and the file system itself: the volume manager that allows virtualizing multiple hard drives as a single volume.

On the top of this abstraction layer, ZFS provides a system of pools, which is a really powerful system of snapshotting (a read-only version of a file system stored on the same volume). The space used by the ZFS snapshots is the delta between the snapshotted version and the current version of the file system (similar to an incremental backup), that allows really small backups of the whole file system.

One of the methods used to ensure the integrity of the data is the checksums in the file system. Each block of data has a checksum that is stored in its parent block pointer that is stored in the block itself. Another method is to use the copy on write method to limit the possibility of creating errors when writing data.

ZFS provides *scrub,* which replaces the traditional *fsck* (file system check) to check the integrity of the data. It has multiple advantages, for example, the ability to run it without having to unmount the file system and check the metadata and the data, unlike fsck that only checks the metadata.

LVM

LVM (or Logical Volume Management) allows you to manage multiple local hard drives as a single volume, in a similar way as ZFS, but on a single server. This technology is supported as a Nova driver, allowing you to provision local hard drives of Nova hosts in instances of this host.

IMAGING

The OpenStack compute service (Nova) stores and accesses two types of instances images: the templates used to create the instances and the snapshots you can take of an instance.

The compute service actually uses the imaging service (Glance) to get and store the data and the details of these images. The image details include the following information:

➤   The displayable name of the image (e.g. Debian Jessie)

➤   The disk format (e.g. QCOW2, RAW)

➤ The size of the image and the minimum resources required to run

➤ The status of the image indicating a potential operation and its availability (e.g. queued, saving, active)

➤ A checksum of the image

The images can be used to create new instances from existing data, and the three main use cases are:

➤ The base images of your infrastructure used to create a new instance and configure it from scratch, using for example a provisioning tool or a configuration management tool (see section 6).

➤ The snapshot you take from an existing instance you can reuse to create an instance with the same configuration, to restore a backup of an instance, or moreover it can be a way to resize an instance (i.e. changing flavor).

➤ Migrate your instance between infrastructures, regions, providers, and even between hypervisors using standard images f ormats.

Where Is It Stored?

The details of the images are stored in a relational database (by default MySQL, which is the default for all OpenStack projects).

The data of the images can be stored in different ways: a local file system (the default storage solution), block storage, and objects storage, or VMware datastores. In fact, the images data can be stored anywhere; the only requirement is to have a backend storage driver implemented to support the operations on the stored data.

The most common way to store the different images of the instances is to use the infrastructure itself to store them: by flattening them as single files (QCOW2, RAW, etc.) and storing them in the object storage service (see Figure 2-7), or to keep them stored as blocks by using the block storage service (Cinder).

FIGURE 2-7

Storing images as blocks can be great if you want to use the same storage infrastructure as the one used by the block storage service and have the ability to directly attach an image without having to download it. In this case the block data will be the exact same one as the original block or the original device data.

If you are using a Ceph infrastructure behind your block storage service or beside your OpenStack infrastructure, you may want to directly use the *Ceph RBD (RADOS Block Device)* driver in Glance. By "behind," we mean that the Ceph infrastructure is abstracted by the Cinder API and used with the Cinder driver. By "beside," we mean that the Ceph infrastructure is not used in

OpenStack, but as a block storage service but can still be used to store the images with Glance. This will avoid you having an extra API between your imaging service and your final storage backend of the images, and potentially it can add the ability to separate your production storage backend used to run your block storage service from your imaging service that will contain your template and snapshot. This could be, for example, different Ceph infrastructures, different *Ceph OSD* (object storage nodes), or different Ceph storage pools with different resources allocated inside of the same infrastructure.

Conversely, you may want to store flatten versions of your images in an object storage service. For example, when using mainly the imaging service to store a lot of snapshots as backups, the image will be simply store as files, allowing you to easily upload and download them without having to create a block device or reading all of the data from a block device to return it over the image service HTTP API. Moreover, you can store images in a format that uses an optimization strategy, which can be great if you generate a lot of download requests on the Imaging API.

If you want to store the images in an external object storage service of your OpenStack infrastructure, you can use the S3 storage driver in Glance to put your images (templates and snapshots) into the *AWS S3* (Amazon Web Services Simple Storage Service). This can be an interesting solution to store some backups of your infrastructure in an external secure service, allowing you to potentially have a disaster recovery plan on *AWS EC2* (Elastic Cloud Computing, the Compute Service from AWS) using the data from your OpenStack infrastructure.

Different Image Formats

Stored images on the imaging service can have different formats, depending upon the ones that are supported by your hypervisor and the features you want to use.

The notion of *image format* includes two different notions: the *disk format*, which corresponds to the real data of the disk image and the *container format* that contains the metadata information of a disk image.

Here are the most used disk formats:

➤ **Raw**: the most simple format possible–an unstructured and exact copy of a device data. This one is usually huge since it needs to allocate the whole image space in a single file, so some parts are unused and empty.

➤ **QCOW2**: stands for *QEMU Copy on Write*. This format uses a strategy to compress the data contained in the image. The allocation of the storage size is delayed until the space is actually required to store the data. Thus this format is flexible since this one can be expanded if some data is added, unlike the *raw* image of a device. Moreover, it is possible to store the additional changes in another file that will contain the difference from the original base QCOW2 image, using the Copy on Write feature provided by this format.

➤ **VHD**: stands for *Virtual Hard Disk*, which is almost standard for the Microsoft technologies (Windows and Hyper-V). For example, it is possible to easily attach a VHD image to a Windows system without having a virtualization engine because the Operating System natively supports this format. A VHD image can be modified directly, thus changing some files, and making a backup or a recovery inside the image.

➤ **VMDK**: the default VMware image format, which is supported by other virtualization solutions like QEMU or VirtualBox. This supports multiple provisioning strategies including the thin provisioning, and allowing provisioning the block only when these ones are written in the image.

The additional information of the images, such as the metadata information, can be stored in external containers if they are not in the image file. In the same way as the images data format, the multiple container format exists and are supported by OpenStack and the virtualization drivers. The most used is the OVF (Open Virtualization Format), an open standard based on an XML descriptor file detailing the packaged virtual machine.

DASHBOARD

OpenStack includes a dashboard project named Horizon, which is a web interface built with the Django framework and the different OpenStack APIs from the OpenStack services.

The Graphical User Interface (GUI) provided by the Horizon dashboard is a great way to get started with OpenStack and its different components. It allows booting your first instance with a simple setup assistant, and then creates your first Swift container, thus managing a few resources (see Figure 2-8).

FIGURE 2-8

Using this GUI can simplify your everyday life if your OpenStack projects are small or use only the main features. It doesn't scale well, however, when you start to have hundreds or thousands of instances and networks, and want to use features that are not considered basic. For example, creating a new network port with a specific configuration and attaching it to an existing instance would not be basic.

The next step is then to use the command line (CLI) or the different OpenStack APIs to administrate your account or infrastructure and start to automate the deployment, management and the use of your OpenStack resources.

Because the command line implements all of the APIs, this is a good way to test all of the features, and discover the API methods, their requests, and response formats before starting to develop and use it in an application. Otherwise this one can be easily scripted to simply automate and repeat your everyday administrative tasks using OpenStack.

NETWORKING

The networking service within OpenStack is responsible for providing network connectivity within the cloud as well as between instances in the cloud and the outside world. OpenStack provides two different networking services. The legacy solution is part of the Nova compute module, and is referred to as nova-network or "Nova networking." The Neutron project provides the new networking solution, and includes much more functionality and flexibility.

Both solutions provide two different types of IP addresses: *private IP addresses* and *floating IP addresses*. The private addresses are the ones that the VMs instances themselves see. That is, running `ip addr` on a Linux VM instance will show you the private address. Instances communicate within the cloud using their private addresses. In OpenStack, each VM will have at least one private IP address, but it doesn't need a floating IP address.

The floating addresses are those available from outside the cloud (and often the public Internet), and are directed to a specific VM instance using the Network Address Translation (NAT). Floating IP addresses may be associated with a VM at the time of its creation, or any time thereafter. They may also be moved to a different VM–this is what makes them "floating" IP addresses. They are not fixed to a specific VM or even tenant, and may be freely moved from one to another.

Another important concept in OpenStack networking is the distinction between *provider networks* and *tenant networks*. Provider networks are objects defined in OpenStack that provide information about a part of the physical network infrastructure, and can only be created by administrators. The cloud administrator creates provider networks within OpenStack that correspond to the physical networks configured within the infrastructure. This allows OpenStack to manage the connectivity between the cloud and the physical network. These networks can be used to provide external access via floating IP addresses, or they can provide VMs with IP addresses on the physical infrastructure subnets (thus avoiding the use of floating IPs for those VMs).

In contrast, ordinary users create tenant networks. These networks are isolated from other tenants, and are under the control of the owner. They may or may not map directly to the underlying physical networks, depending upon the segmentation strategy set up by the cloud administrator. That strategy is defined by the cloud operator and hidden from the tenant. From an application developer's point of view, the particular segmentation strategy is not important. What is important is to understand that the tenant networks are accessible only to the tenant that creates them, except through floating IP addresses.

Nova Networking

Nova networking is deprecated in favor of Neutron networking, but some existing clouds still use it, so having some familiarity with it can be useful.

Nova networking provides a simple networking solution with limited flexibility in the topology and configuration. In particular, tenants have little control over the topology and cannot create complex networking environments.

In most installations, Nova networking will be configured with either a single "flat" network shared by all tenants, or with a VLAN per tenant (See Figure 2-9).

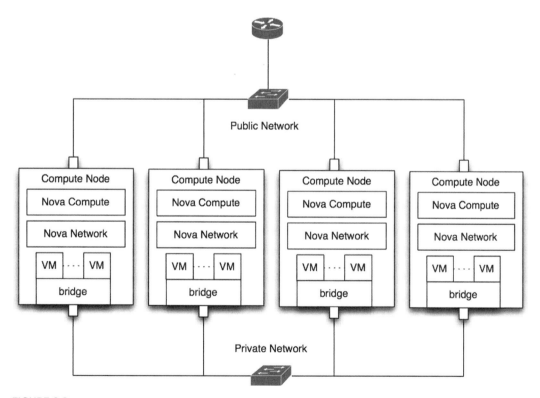

FIGURE 2-9

In Nova networking, as an application developer, you have little control over building out the topology.

Neutron Networking

Neutron networking is the new, standalone networking service within OpenStack. As a software-defined networking solution, it provides the ability to create complex tenant topologies, and it integrates with a wide variety of vendor SDN products. The idea is to be able to reproduce physical network topologies in a completely virtual environment. Just like Nova Compute, which lets you virtualize machine instances, Neutron Networking lets you virtualize networking components such as routers, firewalls, and load balancers, as shown in Figure 2-10.

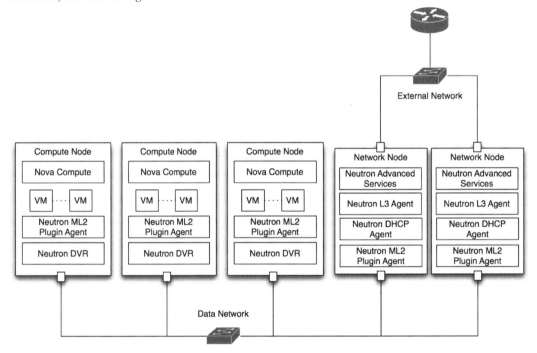

FIGURE 2-10

In Neutron, there are separate Network nodes (shown in Figure 2-10), as opposed to Nova Networking, which relies solely on the compute nodes. The Network nodes handle the advanced services such as Load Balancer-as-a-Service, Firewall-as-a-Service, and Virtual Private Network-as-a-Service. Additionally, they provide the connectivity to the external world outside the cloud. In early versions of Neutron (prior to Juno), all Layer 3 traffic between different subnets went through the network node, even if it was between VMs on the same compute node. Only Layer 2 traffic could transit from directly between the compute nodes, or even within a compute node. In Juno, the Distributed Virtual Router (DVR) functionality was added to provide local routing on the compute node. However, traffic still goes through the network nodes to leave the cloud, or to access advanced services.

How Neutron Helps Applications

Consider deploying a three-tier application in a traditional environment. You need to buy servers, switches, routers, firewalls, load balancers, and SSL offload load balancers–and you'll need them in pairs for redundancy. Each of them needs to be racked, connected in the exact manner needed for the application, and manually configured. You'll need to plan out the space, power, and cooling needs created by the new application. Even if you virtualize the servers, you still need to setup all of the networking gear. This requires a lot of expense in capital equipment as well as a lot of time for setup.

> **A PRACTICAL NOTE** *In practice, you wouldn't use all of this equipment. Modern network devices can serve several of these purposes, either directly or through service modules. In that case you can use VLAN tagging to create isolated segments, so from a security perspective it is equivalent. However, even in that case, Figure 2-11 illustrates the complexity of this deployment, as each of these services still needs manual configuration.*

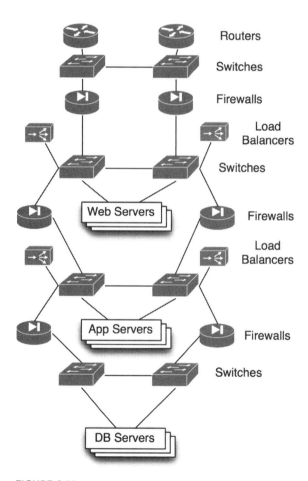

Routers

Switches

Firewalls

Load Balancers

Switches

Web Servers

Firewalls

Load Balancers

App Servers

Firewalls

Switches

DB Servers

FIGURE 2-11

In a software-defined world, all of that complexity moves to the software layer. At the hardware layer, we have uniform racks of servers, with top-of-rack switches, typically connected to a *spine-and-leaf* networking fabric (see Figure 2-12).

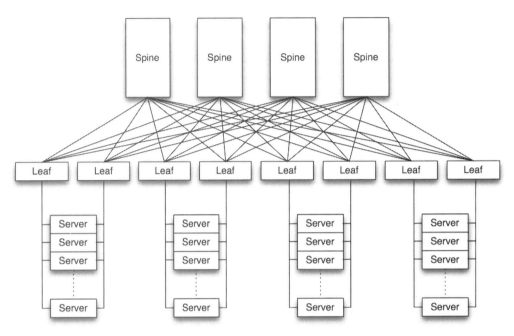

FIGURE 2-12

The servers here are the compute, network, storage and other physical nodes in your cloud. The leaves are the top-of-rack switches that all of these plug into. The spines aggregate all of the traffic from the leaves, and every leaf can reach every other leaf with just two hops, since every leaf connects to every spine. Additionally, inter-leaf traffic can be spread across the spines without taking a longer path. This helps reduce bottlenecks. In this layout, you still have full redundancy as each server is dually connected to two leaves.

None of the hardware layer changes are based upon application deployments, as long as there is capacity. And when there is a change, you can add a servers or racks in a simple and consistent way, without having to know anything about the applications that will be running on them.

As new applications are provisioned and decommissioned, there is no longer a need to rack, cable and configure specific hardware devices for those applications. Networks are overlaid on top of the consistent hardware via automation and pure software-based network devices. You create virtual routers, load balancers, and firewalls in software, and connect them via API calls. This can dramatically cut down on the time it takes to deploy an application, as well as enable repeatable, template-based deployment.

Of course, software may not perform as well as specialized hardware. Additionally, there are many features that the standard OpenStack reference implementation doesn't support. Neutron provides a rich set of pluggable interfaces to address these concerns. These plugins enable third-party vendors to integrate directly into the Neutron service, extending its functionality. Plugins can interact with external SDN controllers or existing physical networking gear, provide advanced services such as VPN-as-a-Service, or integrate with external IP Address Management platforms. The difference between this and setting up a traditional network for an application, though, is that it is still all done with the same, simple APIs, rather than through vendor-specific proprietary configuration protocols.

Understanding Core Neutron Objects

The Neutron object model consists of some familiar analogs with the physical world, such as ports, subnets, and routers. There are also some logical concepts that really only exist in OpenStack, such as subnet pools and address scopes.

A Neutron *network* corresponds to a Layer 2 broadcast domain. If you're not that familiar with networking, in the physical world you can think of this as essentially a single "wire" for nodes to talk over. Layer 2 deals exclusively with MAC addresses–there is no need for IP addresses in this layer. Switches provide optimizations on top of the "single wire" model by forwarding Ethernet frames down only the necessary links. They also provide VLANs–or Virtual Local Area Networks–which allow you to divide a single switch into multiple broadcast domains. Essentially, you get to say which ports "go together". In Neutron, the network model captures this concept.

A Neutron *subnet* provides the Layer 3 connectivity. That is, it provides the IP addressing and enables Neutron routers to pass traffic between Neutron networks. This is very similar to the standard networking model. A subnet is associated with a particular Layer 2 network, and a Neutron *router* is used to interconnect subnets, just like in the physical world.

In Neutron, when creating a router you can additionally specify that it provide high availability (HA), or that it be a distributed virtual router, which as mentioned above is spread out across all of the compute nodes. DVR is a more recent implementation than the standard router, and as such has some limitations. As of the Kilo release, DVR does not work with FWaaS for east-west (between VM) traffic. Also, it requires compute nodes to have a public IP to handle distributed floating IP addresses.

A Neutron *port* is associated with a network. Its analog in the real world is an actual switch port where you would plug in an Ethernet cable. It is the point of attachment to a network. Neutron will provide Nova with a port to "plug in" the instance interface. One distinction though between the real world and Neutron is that in Neutron a port is also automatically associated with one or more IP addresses (one for each subnet on the network). This is a blurring of the Layer 2 and Layer 3 semantics, and may be resolved in a later release of Neutron.

A Neutron *security group* provides simple, firewall-like functionality. Rules may be defined for ingress and egress traffic, and those rules will be applied at the Neutron port. There is a default security group that will allow traffic between instances in that group, and traffic outbound from instances in the group (egress traffic), but it restricts all inbound traffic. You can utilize the Firewall-as-a-Service project for more sophisticated features.

The Kilo release of Neutron added another concept that is more abstract than those described previously–the *subnet pool*. A subnet pool is a collection of IP network prefixes from which a tenant may allocate subnets. That is, in Juno and earlier, the tenant had to specify a specific subnet–like 10.10.10.0/24–to allocate. In Kilo, the cloud administrator can create a subnet pool–say 10.10.0.0/16–from which the tenant can ask for "any subnet" of a particular size. This way, the tenant really does not need to figure out ahead of time what the subnet should be–they can just ask the subnet pool to figure it out. For example, without subnet pools, you would use this API call to create a new subnet:

```
neutron subnet-create private-network 10.1.0.0/24
```

This requires the caller to know that 10.1.0.0/24 is a valid, available subnet that can be used. With subnet pools, the administrator can create a pool for specific uses–say, for web servers. This pool contains a wide range of addresses from which to allocate subnets, as well as a default prefix length (the "/24" above, which corresponds to the subnet mask). So, instead of the above, you can execute a simpler command:

```
neutron subnet-create private-network -subnetpool web-pool
```

This completely separates the decisions about IP address and subnet allocation from the subnet creation process. This, along with the Pluggable IP Address Management feature added in Liberty, is critical to using clouds in larger organizations that have different groups managing IP space and applications.

In Liberty, one more concept is added, called an *address scope*. This represents a unique Layer 3 address space. In Neutron, you can create the same subnet CIDR (for example, 10.0.0.0/24) on two different networks. This can lead to overlapping IP addresses. This is perfectly valid in Neutron, except that you cannot connect those two networks to the same router. If you did, then Neutron would not be able to distinguish between the same IP address on each network. The address scope generalizes this, providing an object within Neutron to represent the address space to which a subnet belongs. By doing this, Neutron enables better control over routing, and prevents multiple users from accidentally creating overlapping space. It also lets Neutron know when Network Address Translation (NAT) may be needed even between non-overlapping subnets–this can prevent accidental overlap between other subnets on the router.

Understanding Overlay Networks

One of the key features provided by Neutron is the concept of overlay networks. An overlay network is just a segmentation, or segregation, of the network traffic that rides on the physical network. The key part is that from the point of view of the VM, there is a single, ordinary network. But in fact, this is an illusion created by Neutron, since the data is actually moving across various physical boundaries in the data center. For example, when a VM sends out a Layer 2 broadcast such as an ARP request, that request may be packaged up and sent across the physical network to several different compute nodes. Then, it is unwrapped on those nodes and delivered to each VM on the same overlay network. It is overlay networks that provide the ability to separate tenant traffic, enabling us to share the underlying physical infrastructure and thus make full use of it (See Figure 2-13).

The simplest and most familiar form of an overlay network is the VLAN. A VLAN tags Ethernet frames with a 12-bit number, and this enables the physical networking gear to differentiate between the traffic that belongs with individual VLANs. When a user creates a tenant network in Neutron, it can be assigned a particular VLAN tag, and Neutron can then keep all of that traffic segregated from other traffic within the network.

A big drawback, however, is that a 12-bit tag provides at most 4096 VLANs. In a large multi-tenant cloud, there may be many more separate networks required. Other technologies have been developed to address this gap. The two you will see in OpenStack's reference implementation are Virtual Extensible Local Area Network (VXLAN) and Generic Routing Encapsulation (GRE). While VLANs are based on Layer 2 technology–they tag Ethernet frames–these two technologies are based upon Layer 3 technology. That is, they work by encapsulating the data in IP packets rather than by tagging Ethernet frames. This can allow the overlay networks to stretch across larger networks.

Additionally, the VXLAN protocol provides a 24-bit number to differentiate networks, allowing over 16 million distinct overlay networks.

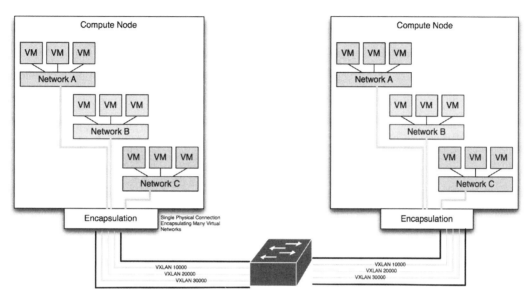

FIGURE 2-13

BRINGING IT ALL TOGETHER

To help understand how these different pieces interact, let's step through what happens when you launch a VM and see how all of the pieces fit together. This is a simplified workflow that the user and the various services will go through in a typical case of launching a VM with ephemeral storage only (i.e., the storage and all disk contents go away when the VM is terminated). Many internal steps are glossed over here, since the focus is on the interaction between the services.

In order to boot any VM, you'll need to prepare a few things first. For this example, we will use the individual service CLI clients. There is also a general `openstack` client but it does not offer all of the features of the separate service clients.

First, you need to decide on the flavor of the VM you want. The flavor represents the combination of CPUs, memory, and storage for the VM. The flavors can be retrieved from Nova (some columns omitted for brevity):

```
$ nova flavor-list
+----+-----------+-----------+------+-----------+------+-------+
| ID | Name      | Memory_MB | Disk | Ephemeral | Swap | VCPUs |
+----+-----------+-----------+------+-----------+------+-------+
| 1  | m1.tiny   | 512       | 1    | 0         |      | 1     |
| 2  | m1.small  | 2048      | 20   | 0         |      | 1     |
| 3  | m1.medium | 4096      | 40   | 0         |      | 2     |
| 4  | m1.large  | 8192      | 80   | 0         |      | 4     |
```

```
| 42 | m1.nano   | 64    | 0   | 0 |   |   | 1 |   |
| 5  | m1.xlarge | 16384 | 160 | 0 |   |   | 8 |   |
| 84 | m1.micro  | 128   | 0   | 0 |   |   | 1 |   |
+----+-----------+-----------+------+-----------+------+-------+
$
```

We will use m1.tiny.

Next, you need to know what *image* to use. The image contains the bootable operating system for the VM. Until we need to actually build an application, examples in this book will generally use CirrOS (https://launchpad.net/cirros), which is a very small, minimal OS that is useful for testing of the cloud platform. If you are following along, then other images may be available on your OpenStack instance. Choose a small one for experimentation.

```
$ glance image-list
+---------+------------------------------+...+----------+--------+
| ID      | Name                         |...| Size     | Status |
+---------+------------------------------+...+----------+--------+
| 6d...e0 | cirros-0.3.4-x86_64-uec      |...| 25165824 | active |
| 5f...92 | cirros-0.3.4-x86_64-uec-kernel  |...| 4979632  | active |
| 06...c6 | cirros-0.3.4-x86_64-uec-ramdisk |...| 3740163  | active |
+---------+------------------------------+...+----------+--------+
$
```

Since we want to be able to access our instance over the network, rather than just via the console, you need to attach it to a network. So, call the Neutron service to find out the available networks.

```
$ neutron net-list
+---------+---------+------------------------------------------------------------+
| id      | name    | subnets                                                    |
+---------+---------+------------------------------------------------------------+
| 50...56 | public  | 09c872aa-02fa-4e81-9cb1-846399938c64 2001:db8::/64         |
|         |         | b9d882f3-8378-42cc-b5fa-4cb2576c7fb4 192-168.20.0/25       |
| fa...ea | private | 5bd94138-3a4a-4966-b216-b4530a0f489d fddc:b6e3:ede0::/64   |
|         |         | ece9ba64-cf28-424c-8187-8df763301a56 10.0.0.0/24           |
+---------+---------+------------------------------------------------------------+
```

Now we have everything Nova needs to know at boot time, so we simply run the nova boot command (output has been abbreviated).

```
$ nova boot -flavor m1.tiny -image cirros-0.3.4-x86_64-uec \
         -nic net-id=fa3282e4-64ba-44fa-9644-46da784234ea i-1
+------------------------------------+------------------------------------------+
| Property                           | Value                                    |
+------------------------------------+------------------------------------------+
|                                    |                                          |
| OS-EXT-STS:power_state             | 0                                        |
| OS-EXT-STS:task_state              | scheduling                               |
| OS-EXT-STS:vm_state                | building                                 |
| OS-SRV-USG:launched_at             | -                                        |
| OS-SRV-USG:terminated_at           | -                                        |
| created                            | 2015-07-24T05:52:20Z                     |
| flavor                             | m1.tiny (1)                              |
| id                                 | a9d9e891-e85a-471b-9844-cd3eda0659a0     |
```

```
| image            | cirros-0.3.4-x86_64-uec (6d...e0)    |
| key_name         | -                                    |
| metadata         | {}                                   |
| name             | i-1                                  |
| progress         | 0                                    |
| security_groups  | default                              |
| status           | BUILD                                |
| tenant_id        | 56082fc3830e43d4af307bed5d1d5f90     |
| updated          | 2015-07-24T05:52:20Z                 |
| user_id          | e749c12a525d4b259e0e291fd91ca53a     |
+--------------------------------------+--------------------------------------+
$
```

So what does Nova do when we initiate the boot command? First, it validates our credentials with Keystone, to make sure we have the authority to launch the VM. After that, the boot process is a state machine that takes the instance state from BUILD to ACTIVE under normal circumstances. Nova first stores the instance in the database with Status BUILD and Task State scheduling. The primary Status remains BUILD, so to see the progress of the boot we need to look at the secondary Task Status. Both statuses are tracked in the Nova database.

```
$ nova list
+----------+------+--------+------------+-------------+--------------+
| ID       | Name | Status | Task State | Power State | Networks     |
+----------+------+--------+------------+-------------+--------------+
| a9...a0  | i-1  | BUILD  | scheduling | NOSTATE     |              |
+----------+------+--------+------------+-------------+--------------+
```

Next, nova sends a request to the Nova scheduler (running on the controller node) via the message queue. It is the scheduler's job to figure out the physical compute node on which to run the instance. It will select a node based upon the characteristics of the VM–how much CPU and memory it needs, for example–and the available capacity of each host. It will then post a request back to the message queue that includes the selected host. The command results above show the scheduling state, however, in practice scheduling will likely be fast enough that you won't catch it in that state.

Nova picks the scheduled instance request off the queue and updates the database, then sends a message across the queue again – this time to the nova-compute process that sits on the selected compute host. The nova compute agent makes a RESTful API call to the Glance image service to retrieve the image.

Each time one service talks to another, Keystone may be invoked to validate the token (the details depend on the type of token). In this case, Glance would verify that the user has permission to the selected image. If so, Nova downloads the image to its image cache.

Now the host is selected and the image is available on that host. But Nova still needs to know how to connect the instance to a network. It sets the task status to networking, and then calls the Neutron networking service to create a *port*. The port can be thought of just like a real, physical switch port. It provides a place to "plug in" the instance network interface to the virtual switching fabric. Again, this between-service interaction is done via the same RESTful APIs that other clients use. In fact, we could have created the port ahead of time, and provided a port_id to Nova instead of a network_id.

Neutron creates the port and allocates and IP address on a subnet associated with the supplied `network_id`. Like Nova, Neutron has agents running on each compute node. It is on that node that it will create the virtual port.

Finally Nova takes all of this information, sets the task status to `spawning`, and calls the hypervisor (KVM by default) to actually spin up the instance.

SUMMARY

In this chapter you learned in detail about the core components of OpenStack and how they work together to create a cloud. Finally, you put it all together to understand the details of how Nova interacts with Keystone, Neutron, Glance, and Cinder to spin up virtual machines. These are the basic services you will find in most OpenStack clouds, but there are a host of other services. In the next chapter, we will look at some of the less core–but still important–services offered in some OpenStack clouds.

3

Understanding the OpenStack Ecosystem: Additional Projects

WHAT'S IN THIS CHAPTER?

- ➤ Understanding Cloud Orchestration

- ➤ Orchestration capabilities in OpenStack

- ➤ OpenStack Heat in details

- ➤ Software-defined-storage (SDS)

- ➤ Cloud databases as a use case of SDS

- ➤ Cloud databases: maintain or consume

- ➤ OpenStack Database as a Service: Trove

- ➤ A look at Magnum and Containers as a Service

- ➤ Coverage of Murano and Ceilometer

The core components discussed in Chapter 2 cover the basic IaaS functionality of OpenStack. Just using those features, OpenStack enables you to set up and run applications. However, there is more to building, deploying, and supporting an application than is covered in those components. This chapter will discuss additional OpenStack projects that enable you to define repeatable application deployments on VMs or containers, make those applications available via DNS, and monitor the virtual infrastructure on which those applications are hosted. Although these aren't labeled as orchestration, such applications also require manual configuration and deployment in some manner. This chapter will cover how to use OpenStack to manage container-based applications, how to package applications for use by others, and how to take advantage of the Database-as-a-Service feature to shift more complexity from your application to the cloud infrastructure.

DEMO APPLICATION SOURCE CODE

You can access the source code from our demo application via GitHub: `https://github.com/johnbelamaric/openstack-appdev-book`.

OPENSTACK HEAT

In cloud computing theory, it is well known that there is more than one type of service. One of the most popular and interesting (in terms of flexibility) services is the Platform-as-a-Service (PaaS), which allows you to tap into cloud capabilities in different ways, such as with a cloud orchestration service. Let's take a look at the scientific definition of cloud orchestration:

➤ It provides you with the ability to control and arrange a set of underlying technology infrastructures (hardware and hypervisor). You can match the intended commands inputted by the users to create a set of automated events that deliver the request with the maximum efficiency (source: `http://howtobuildacloud.com/cloud-enablement/cloud-orchestration-starts-to-play-its-tune/`)

➤ It provides you with the ability to manage, coordinate, and provision all parts of a customer solution automatically, with no administrative intervention, ideally from a self-service interface. This is much like a conductor who conducts an orchestra making sure that all of the instruments/performers are in tune and in time (source: `https://www.flexiant.com/`).

Putting definitions aside, the most important point of cloud orchestration services is not what they are, but what they do. As a cloud consumer, a provider, or a reseller of cloud services, all that matters is that cloud orchestration makes your cloud consumption experience better. If you are looking for some service or capability that will make your cloud application resources more scalable, instantly deployable, efficient, simpler to use, and easier to bill and manage, you are looking at cloud orchestration service capabilities.

You may question the idea that an orchestration service is a platform service, but cloud orchestrators were the first services that gave us an ability to consume/operate cloud resources in a pre-defined way (specific DSL) within a single API specification (just remember old days, when you had to learn tons of API specs to accomplish your business needs).

Orchestration Capabilities in OpenStack

So, cloud orchestration is something that you can't live without, but what about OpenStack? Can you say the same thing? Let's examine the OpenStack orchestration service, called Heat.

Heat is the main project in the OpenStack orchestration program. It implements an orchestration engine to launch multiple composite cloud applications based upon templates in the form of text files that can be treated like code. A native Heat template format is evolving, but Heat also provides the compatibility with the AWS CloudFormation template format. This allows many existing CloudFormation templates to be launched on OpenStack. Heat provides both an OpenStack-native REST API and a CloudFormation-compatible Query API (source: `https://wiki.openstack.org/wiki/Heat`).

OpenStack Heat in Details

Let's examine what Heat can do for you. Below you can see a list of template types that Heat supports:

➤ **HOT:** (Heat Orchestration Template). HOT templates are a new generation of templates that aren't backwards-compatible with AWS CloudFormation templates, and can only be used with OpenStack (DSL for HOT—YAML).

➤ **CFN:** Short for AWS CloudFormation. This type was initially supported since Heat's first releases (DSL for CFN-JSON).

Each template defines infrastructure resource requirements, the relationship between each of the resources, and any software configuration necessary in order to manage a complete application resource lifecycle.

Before looking at a template it is necessary to understand a few terms: stack, resource, parameter, and output.

➤ **Stack:** a collection of objects described by a template with its relationships/dependencies that will be deployed in the cloud. stack includes instances (VMs), networking, block storage, object storage buckets, and auto-scaling rules.

➤ **Resource:** an element of stack. For example, VM, security group, subnet, and block storage are the resources of stack.

➤ **Parameters:** these are tidbits of information, like a specific image ID, flavor, volume size, or a particular network ID that is passed to the Heat template by the user. In general cases, templates are parameterized to allow some flavor of flexibility, yet in common cases it is up to the user. The general application of parameters lays in configuring resources. For example, if you need to deploy a virtual machine (VM) resource, you have to explicitly define the flavor and the image ID. These are parameters for resources and in the template it is possible to have a huge section for parameters in real life. Parameters are not a mandatory thing, however, but it is possible that the resource definition puts some default values in resource configuration.

➤ **Outputs:** this is interesting, since in common cases it outputs a fully custom data structure that is being defined at the end of a successful deployment. Let's just review a small example. Let's say you have three resources: VM, security group with rules, and software deployment. The idea here is to deploy a VM with software in it (Nodecellar, Wordpress, MySql or whatever) and we need to restrict the access to that deployed application. This deployment configuration assumes that we're deploying a PaaS application and users are able to access it within specific connection strings. Here are the template outputs: once deployment is ready, Heat will try to get outputs according to its definition from the template using built-in template DSL functions.

Now it's time to take a look at a real-life example of a Heat template:

```
heat_template_version: 2013-05-23

description: >
  A HOT template that holds a VM instance with an attached
```

```
    Cinder volume.  The VM does nothing, it is only created.

parameters:

  key_name:
    type: string
    description: Name of an existing key pair to use for the instance
    constraints:
      - custom_constraint: nova.keypair
        description: Must name a public key (pair) known to Nova

  flavor:
    type: string
    description: Flavor for the instance to be created
    default: m1.small
    constraints:
      - custom_constraint: nova.flavor
        description: Must be a flavor known to Nova

  image:
    type: string
    description: >
      Name or ID of the image to use for the instance.
      You can get the default from
      http://cloud.fedoraproject.org/fedora-20.x86_64.qcow2
      There is also
      http://cloud.fedoraproject.org/fedora-20.i386.qcow2
      Any image should work since this template
      does not ask the VM to do anything.
    constraints:
      - custom_constraint: glance.image
        description: Must identify an image known to Glance

  network:
    type: string
    description: The network for the VM
    default: private

  vol_size:
    type: number
    description: The size of the Cinder volume
    default: 1

resources:

  my_instance:
    type: OS::Nova::Server
    properties:
      key_name: { get_param: key_name }
      image: { get_param: image }
      flavor: { get_param: flavor }
```

```
        networks: [{network: {get_param: network} }]

    my_vol:
      type: OS::Cinder::Volume
      properties:
        size: { get_param: vol_size }

    vol_att:
      type: OS::Cinder::VolumeAttachment
      properties:
        instance_uuid: { get_resource: my_instance }
        volume_id: { get_resource: my_vol }
        mountpoint: /dev/vdb

outputs:
  instance_networks:
    description: The IP addresses of the deployed instance
    value: { get_attr: [my_instance, networks] }
```

As you can see, this template was written using HOT DSL, and here is the list of parameters:

- `key_name`
- `flavor`
- `image`
- `network`
- `vol_size`

And here is the list of resources:

- `my_instance`
- `my_vol`
- `vol_attr`

Here are the stack outputs (as you can see now, HOT DSL provides a set of functions to retrieve specific resource attributes or get deployment parameters):

- `instance_networks`

Let's figure out what this template does. It deploys a VM, provisions a block storage (data volume), attaches volume to the VM, and as part of the output, it returns an IP address of the VM. As for OpenStack operators, let's examine the architecture of Heat (see Figure 3-1):

- **heat-api** is an OpenStack-native RESTful API. This component processes API requests by sending them to the Heat engine service via AMQP.

- **heat-api-cfn** is similar to the CloudFormation-compatible RESTful API.

- **heat-engine** provides the main orchestration functionality.

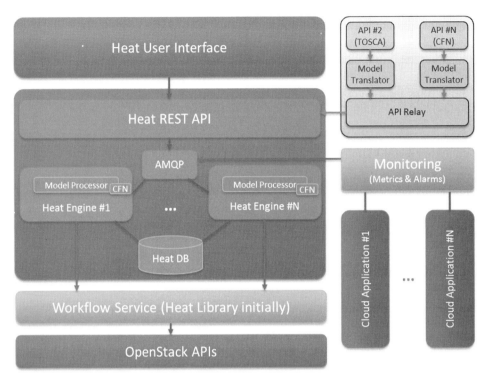

FIGURE 3-1

This chapter is not about the hands-on best practices for deploying Heat into your OpenStack environment. You've seen what Heat can do, though, and how it can do it. If you are interested in developing or consuming Heat, it is necessary to learn its API and technology stack.

Let's sum up what we've learned about orchestration in OpenStack. It has a rich ecosystem of modules available to facilitate automation throughout all stages of the stack's resources and their lifecycle, resulting in greatly reduced time-to-market for many IT demands/projects. Heat is the leading orchestration tool for OpenStack-based clouds, and it is an official part of the OpenStack distribution. With strong enterprise support and substantial on-going contribution, Heat is fast becoming the great tool of choice for OpenStack private and public clouds.

OPENSTACK DATABASE AS A SERVICE: TROVE

We have covered orchestration in the cloud and how it can help your business. Let's spend some time covering the differences between creating applications in and out of a cloud. As a software architect you need to give everyone the basic idea of how your application should be deployed and how it should work, especially in a cloud infrastructure. In general, you need a persistent storage for your app—you need a database. So, what cloud can give that to you? Would that be a cloud database or just Infrastructure-as-a-Service (IaaS)?

Cloud Database As Use Case of Software-Defined-Storage (SDS)

You may wonder if Heat is able to be the software that defines storage with the help of its DSL. This is true, but it is necessary to have an ability to manage storage in a very specific way. For example, given that software should enable a software-defined storage environment, it may also provide policy management for feature options such as deduplication, replication, clustering, fault-tolerance, thin provisioning, snapshots, and backup.

In the case of Heat, it is pretty complicated to provide all of these capabilities, since it would make cloud orchestration very complicated and hardly maintainable. That is why you should use Heat or implement your own orchestration, since a custom engine for services will do the storage provisioning. Within OpenStack, you can find a big variety of services that do storage provisioning: Cinder, Swift, and Manila.

Speaking of persistent storage, as a developer you need to have the capability of delivering a database as a specific use case of software-defined storage. This is great having a service that uses database delivery using concepts of SDS, and taking all deployments and maintaining them behind the scene.

A cloud database is a database that typically runs on a cloud computing platform, in our case that is OpenStack, and provides limited access, allowing users to interact with the database through its native API. For a long period of time there were no cloud databases, so database consumers tried to deal with it in their own way. There are two common deployment models: users can run databases on the cloud independently, using a pre-configured virtual machine image, or they can purchase access proprietary solutions that are working above different cloud platforms. So what's the problem with the last approach?

OpenStack and Trove

There are problems with using proprietary solutions that are working on different cloud platforms. It is not enough to buy a product, since within some period of time the product must be supported. And if you are aware of software services and software product business models, you would definitely choose a service that provides databases instead of developing and supporting your own custom solution. This is because it seems that products always cost less because of a one-time purchase and no support, yet every problem is your personal headache, and support for products in general becomes more expensive than the cost of the product. On the other hand, purchasing a service subscription takes less money due to its time access restrictions, but in the case of software services support, it is being handled by the service provider.

Note that the first cloud database service was provided by Amazon AWS, called Amazon RDBS. It is only relational, NoSQL not even once, but when RDBS was released, NoSQL was not widely available, so Amazon AWS customers were completely satisfied by SQL databases. Currently, RDBS is still alive and popular, and nothing much has changed (new flavors of databases were added, which are a replication for MySQL).

Enterprises need clusters and datacenters full of clusters, and they need them as quickly as possible. So, here are our demands: we need new SQL/NoSQL solutions, we need clusters, and we need automated management operations (see SDS capabilities), and finally, we need it all in OpenStack by the end of today. So, OpenStack definitely missed such abilities, primarily the way to declare storage as a database using a specific language. There are a couple of possible ways to accomplish database installation within OpenStack:

➤ Firstboot.d or cloud-init

➤ Chef

➤ Puppet

➤ Ansible

➤ Post-provisioning scripts execution with fabric

It is easy to deploy a database. But what about the cost of your time to automate management tasks? If you choose this path, eventually you would end up spending time/money to update your scripts to adopt them to new requirements.

Obviously, enterprise customers would love to consume services and resources instead of maintaining them. Custom and very specific solutions may not work in terms of SDS, however, since SDS DSL should be flexible. So, we need a service for databases that meet the concepts of SDS. Let's go back to 2012. Rackspace and HP decided to collaborate and implement such a service for OpenStack: OpenStack database service, Trove.

Before describing the concepts of Trove itself, please keep in mind that Trove is not a database. Even if it was defined as a database as a service, Trove is not a database. Trove is a tool that delivers and manages database instances in a cloud environment. OpenStack's Database as a Service (DBaaS) project is in active development but holds a real treasure. This service is designed to provide all of the goods of both SQL and NoSQL databases without the hassle of having to handle complex administrative tasks. It is necessary to have a dedicated service that completely implements all SDS management operations. The idea was to provide a scalable and reliable cloud database as a service provisioning functionality for both relational and non-relational database engines, and to continue to improve its fully-featured and extensible open source framework (including replication, clustering, backup, restore, user/databases CRUD operations).

So, what are those differences between Trove and Amazon RDBS? Trove does NoSQL bootstrapping, however, starting with the Juno release Trove does replication for MySQL and Percona 5.5, as well as sharded clustering for MongoDB 2.x.x.

OpenStack DBaaS In Detail

Let's define what Trove is. In cloud computing there are two definitions for cloud databases: a datasource API service and a data plane API service. Let's take a close look at the cloud pioneer, Amazon. Amazon AWS provides two different types of database services: Amazon RDBS and Amazon DynamoDB (and SimpleDB, the cheap version of DynamoDB). Both of these services are database services, and both deal with databases, but in completely different ways:

➤ **Amazon RDBS:** a data plane API service that deploys databases within a single account. This is best for deployment on demand.

➤ **Amazon DynamoDB:** a datasource API service that creates schema entities over pre-deployed NoSQL database clusters.

From this perspective Trove is not a database. Trove is instead a database instance delivery service. Trove does instant database deployment on demand.

Before looking at Trove's API, you need to understand a few terms that Trove uses.

➤ **Datastore:** a data structure that describes a set of datastore versions, which consists of:

➤ **ID:** simple auto-generated UUID

➤ **Name:** user-defined attribute; actual name of a datastore

➤ **Default datastore Versions ID**

➤ Example: Mysql, Cassandra, Redis, etc.

➤ **Datastore Version:** a data structure that describes a version of a specific database pinned to datastore, which consists of:

➤ **ID:** simple auto-generated UUID

➤ **Datastore ID:** reference to datastore

➤ **Name:** user-defined attribute; actual name of a database version

➤ **Datastore manager:** trove-guestagent manager that is used for datastore management

➤ **Image ID:** reference to a specific Glance image ID

➤ **Packages:** database distribution packages that would be deployed onto a datastore VM

➤ **Active:** boolean flag that defines if a version can be used for instance deployment or not

➤ Example: Name - 5.6

➤ Packages: mysql-server=5.5, percona-xtrabackup=2.1

So, both of these terms are describing which database flavor version should be deployed.

Also it is necessary to understand which images should be used. Unfortunately, Trove is not able to work with pure cloud-ready images due to its architectural specialties—each Glance image should contain Trove's guest agent (an RPC service that manages a database instance where it was installed). For more information on how to create images for Trove, please take a look at this document: `https://github.com/openstack/trove/blob/master/doc/source/dev/building_guest_images.rst`.

Now it is time to proceed to Trove's API and what it can do:

➤ Database instance management (within supported datastores)

➤ Database backup/restore (for MySQL and Percona it is also supported to create an incremental backup)

➤   Post-provisioning configuration management

➤   Clustering (starting with the Juno release for MongoDB 2.x.x, VerticaDB)

➤   Replication (from MySQL and Percona)

➤   Users/database CRUD operations (note, when this book was written not all supported data-store drivers in Trove were able to provide such ability)

Let's take a precise look at Trove's workflow and which OpenStack services are involved with instance provisioning. In Figure 3-2 you can see important Trove elements.

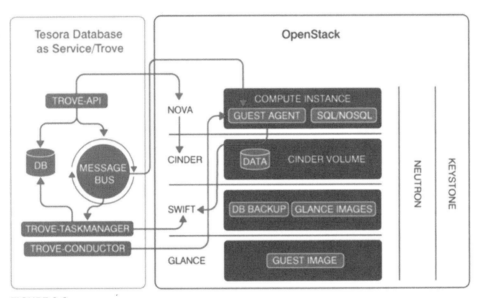

FIGURE 3-2

It is necessary to explain what happens when a user submits an instance provisioning task to Trove. First of all, we have to deal with how each new instance is a new VM with an attached block storage. So, there is no bare metal (say goodbye to Oracle and its license), and no containers. Secondly, for provisioning, Trove requires special images with additional software, which will be described later in this chapter.

So, each time a user creates an instance, Trove does the following:

➤   Nova VM bootstrap

➤   Cinder block storage provisioning

Once the VM is ready and the volume provisioned, Trove sends over an AMQP RPC message to the Trove agent that is being deployed at the VM to setup the database. So, if it's not installed, install it, do additional configuration, and report that the database is ready. You probably noted that Trove does its own orchestration, so this is a community decision. For now Trove doesn't support fully Heat-based provisioning. In Figure 3-3 you can see CLI calls to Trove for instance creation using python-troveclient.

```
$ trove create source-mysql-database 2 --size 2 --datastore mysql
+-------------------+------------------------------------------+
| Property          | Value                                    |
+-------------------+------------------------------------------+
| created           | 2015-08-07 10:57:46                      |
| datastore         | mysql                                    |
| datastore_version | 5.6                                      |
| flavor            | 2                                        |
| id                | f90de567-397c-4d87-a0f1-3f3986ea6784     |
| name              | source-mysql-database                    |
| status            | BUILD                                    |
| updated           | 2015-08-07 10:57:46                      |
| volume            | 2                                        |
+-------------------+------------------------------------------+
```

FIGURE 3-3

Database Backup

Now let's take a look at how the instance backup procedure is implemented. Once a user submits a backup request, it asks its agent to perform a backup. Depending upon its implementation backup, it can be online or off-line. So, the agent uses native database tools to perform backups (xtrabackup for MySQL flavors, nodetool for Cassandra, etc.). Once backup is ready, the agent packages it into an archive and then sends it to remote bucket storage: Swift. In terms of security concerns the agent encrypts the backup using an AES block cipher. But there's a problem. All instances are using the same AES key within any deployment. In Figure 3-4 you can see CLI calls for backing up to Trove using python-troveclient (https://pypi.python.org/pypi/python-troveclient/1.2.0).

```
$ trove backup-create f90de567-397c-a0f1-3f3986ea6784 --description backup_for_f90de567-397c-a0f1-3f3986ea6784
+-------------+----------------------------------------------------------------------------------------------+
| Property    | Value                                                                                        |
+-------------+----------------------------------------------------------------------------------------------+
| created     | 2015-08-07 10:57:46                                                                          |
| datastore   | {'version': '5.6', 'type': 'mysql', 'version_id': '5c0a45c2-e911-4ef3-a3a6-e027cba4bd6f'}    |
| description | backup_for_f90de567-397c-a0f1-3f3986ea6784                                                   |
| id          | 1948f7b6-e369-47de-8688-3bfd8fe24b36                                                         |
| instance_id | f90de567-397c-a0f1-3f3986ea6784                                                              |
| name        | backup_for_f90de567-397c-a0f1-3f3986ea6784                                                   |
| size        | 5.2                                                                                          |
| status      | BUILDING                                                                                     |
| updated     | 2015-08-07 10:57:46                                                                          |
+-------------+----------------------------------------------------------------------------------------------+
```

FIGURE 3-4

Trove Instance Restore

Actually the Trove instance restore is an interesting operation. You should take into account that you can restore data only into a new Trove instance. So, in this key, the restore differs from instance provisioning only by applying a pulled backup from Swift. In Figure 3-5 you can see CLI calls to Trove for restoring a new instance using python-troveclient.

```
$ trove create source-mysql-database-restored 2 --size 2 --datastore mysql --backup 1948f7b6-e369-47de-8688-3bfd8fe24b36
+--------------------+-------------------------------------------+
| Property           | Value                                     |
+--------------------+-------------------------------------------+
| created            | 2015-08-07 10:57:46                        |
| datastore          | mysql                                      |
| datastore_version  | 5.6                                        |
| flavor             | 2                                          |
| id                 | c81f65a5-dc31-4d67-84bc-2bb44196f1cd       |
| name               | source-mysql-database-restored            |
| status             | BUILD                                      |
| updated            | 2015-08-07 10:57:46                        |
| volume             | 2                                          |
+--------------------+-------------------------------------------+
```

FIGURE 3-5

Trove Instance Configuration Management

Taking into account that Trove is a pure PaaS, there's no access to any other services on an instance instead of a database, and there's only one way to manage your instance—through Trove's API. One of the available API endpoints is configuration management that is being deployed. For different types of databases Trove provides an ability to modify different types of configurations. For example, in MySQL flavors it is possible to modify dynamic system variables that are not required to put the database into maintenance mode, but there are also options that require the database service to be shutdown (datadir, logging, etc.). In Figure 3-6 you can see an example of a changing database configuration right after its deployment.

```
$ trove configuration-create configuration_for_f90de567-397c-4d87-a0f1-3f3986ea6784 \
'{"local_infile": 0, "connect_timeout": 120, "collation_server": "latin1_swedish_ci"}' --datastore mysql \
--datastore_version 5.6 --description configuration_for_f90de567-397c-4d87-a0f1-3f3986ea6784
+-------------------------+------------------------------------------------------------------------------------+
| Property                | Value                                                                              |
+-------------------------+------------------------------------------------------------------------------------+
| created                 | 2015-08-07 10:57:46                                                                 |
| datastore_name          | mysql                                                                              |
| datastore_version_id    | 5c0a45c2-e911-4ef3-a3a6-e027cba4bd6f                                               |
| datastore_version_name  | 5.6                                                                               |
| description             | configuration_for_f90de567-397c-4d87-a0f1-3f3986ea6784                             |
| id                      | b9334d6b-b6d6-4d5e-97cc-217c2b722502                                               |
| instance_count          | 0                                                                                 |
| name                    | configuration_for_f90de567-397c-4d87-a0f1-3f3986ea6784                             |
| updated                 | 2015-08-07 10:57:46                                                                 |
| values                  | {"local_infile": 0, "connect_timeout": 120, "collation_server": "latin1_swedish_ci"} |
+-------------------------+------------------------------------------------------------------------------------+
```

FIGURE 3-6

So, you may think that with the help of configuration management you can easily create a replication group for MySQL flavors. Actually, Trove developers did that for you, as shown in Figure 3-7—you can see how Trove addresses replication within its API.

```
$ trove create source-mysql-database-replica 2 --size 2 --datastore mysql --replica_of f90de567-397c-4d87-a0f1-3f3986ea6784
+--------------------+-------------------------------------------+
| Property           | Value                                     |
+--------------------+-------------------------------------------+
| created            | 2015-08-07 10:57:46                        |
| datastore          | mysql                                      |
| datastore_version  | 5.6                                        |
| flavor             | 2                                          |
| id                 | 34b9e5df-f843-418e-9385-97c38f5ac011       |
| name               | source-mysql-database-replica             |
| replica_of         | f90de567-397c-4d87-a0f1-3f3986ea6784       |
| status             | BUILD                                      |
| updated            | 2015-08-07 10:57:46                        |
| volume             | 2                                          |
+--------------------+-------------------------------------------+
```

FIGURE 3-7

Speaking of replication, as part of its replication capabilities, Trove provides an ability to promote slave to master and vice versa (i.e., the demotion). For the sake of stability and predictability it was decided to implement this feature for manual mode only to let users decide whether they want or don't want to do that. Also, starting with the Kilo release Trove is able to perform replication in two different ways (for MySQL flavors): regular binlog replication (binlogs are being transferred through remote storage, by the default—Swift buckets) and a new type of replication that is supported by MySQL 5.6 and greater—GTID replication (see more info at https://dev.mysql.com/doc/refman/5.6/en/replication-gtids-concepts.html).

There's nothing much to say about Trove cluster provisioning. Basically, Trove creates a set of single instances of a specific datastore and its version. Once they are ready, Trove starts to execute operations for each instance to join them into a cluster. The set of operations always follows the industry best practices for cluster bootstrapping (specific to each datastore).

Trove Architecture

Like most OpenStack services Trove itself is divided into multiple services:

➤ **trove-api:** A service that provides a RESTful API that supports JSON to provision and manages Trove instances.

➤ **trove-taskmanage:** A service that does the heavy lifting as far as provisioning instances, managing the lifecycle of instances, and performing operations on the database instance.

➤ **trove-conductor:** A service that is middleware between the guestagent and Trove's backend.

➤ **trove-guestagent:** A VM-site service that manages database instances within its lifecycle.

In Figure 3-8 you can see how Trove's architecture is organized.

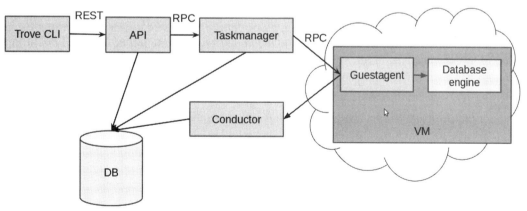

FIGURE 3-8

In the database world, outside of clouds, it is necessary to automate tasks such as a daily backup, but it does seem that Trove misses such ability due to heavy decisions on which technology to pick or creating from scratch. Implementing a scheduler is in the roadmap, but it is not clear when it will happen. So, stepping aside of the community plans, it is obvious that someday Trove's architecture will be extended by that scheduler. So here is the future of its architecture—Figure 3-9 explicitly describes how a scheduler will be integrated.

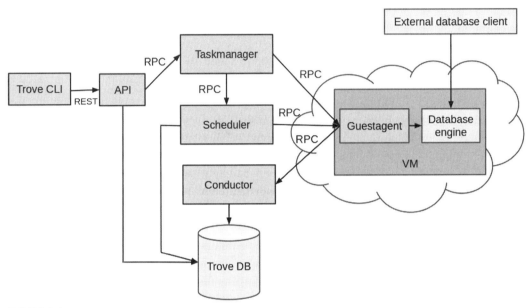

FIGURE 3-9

Here are some last words about Trove. The idea for Trove was to create a competitive (against Amazon AWS or other proprietary solution) service that is part of the OpenStack ecosystem. Yes, it does support the provisioning of multiple database flavors and their versions (datastores with datastore versions in Trove terms). And yes, it does backup/restore for supported databases. It can do clustering for MongoDB and VerticaDB. But are all of these features needed by the enterprise? The answer is yes. And are those supported databases being requested and wanted by the enterprise? Unfortunately no. Trove only partially meets customer needs (at least the upstream version). So OpenStack must support widely used databases such as Oracle 12c, MySQL and others.

DESIGNATE: DNS AS A SERVICE

Being able to quickly deploy virtual machines and applications is the promise of OpenStack and cloud computing in general. However, if it still takes a phone call or service ticket to create a Domain Name Service (DNS) entry for the application, a lot of the effectiveness of automation is lost. That's where DNS-as-a-Service comes into play. It enables application deployments scripts to create DNS zones and records as needed. *Designate* is the project in OpenStack that makes this possible.

Understanding the Designate Architecture

Like other OpenStack services, Designate contains several components: an API end point (`designate-api`), a centralized logical controller (`designate-central`), an internal DNS server (MiniDNS or `designate-mdns`), and a manager (`designate-pool-manager`) to configure downstream, outward-facing DNS servers. There is also an optional `designate-sink` service that watches the message queue and can take other actions as needed based upon fired events (see Figure 3-10).

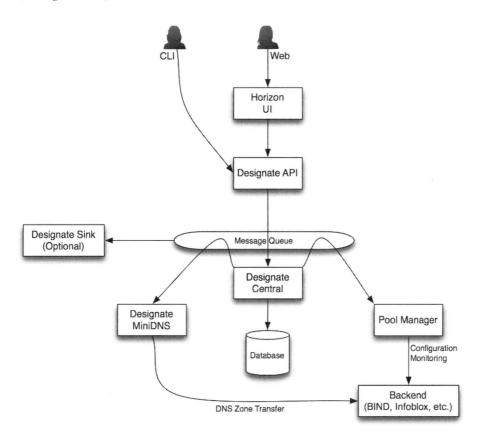

FIGURE 3-10

Designate can be backed by a variety of open source and commercial DNS servers, such as BIND, Infoblox, or PowerDNS. This is not visible to the tenant—the tenant simply has access to APIs to create and manage domains (zones) and the records in those zones. Each of these services is accessed via a "backend" plugin, which contains the specific logic for interacting with that DNS server.

When a user makes a request via Horizon, the CLI client, or the API directly, the request will go to the `designate-api` service. This service manages the inbound HTTP connections, serving up the RESTful API. It communicates with `designate-central` over the message bus.

The `designate-central` service is the hub of activity, coordinating the actions required to carry out the API requests, and managing the persistent storage for the Designate data. When an API call requires a configuration change on one of the backend DNS servers, `designate-central` will send an RPC request to `designate-pool-manager`, which modifies the DNS server configurations. The specifics of what actions it takes will depend on the backend plugin.

When domains or records are created or modified, `designate-central` will also update the `designate-mdns` service. This is a small DNS server that works as a "hidden master" server for all Designate managed domains. That means that it is authoritative for the domain, but it does not show up as an NS record for the domain—in other words, it is hidden from view. Clients cannot find it to directly access it (it's also not accessible externally)—only other name servers can access it. The backend DNS servers, which actually serve requests from clients, are configured to see `designate-mdns` as the primary server, and accept zone transfers from it. DNS zone transfers are a standard DNS method for sharing zone data among servers.

Using Designate

As an application developer, your interaction with Designate will primarily be to create, modify, and delete zones and records. Let's look at the designate CLI client and how to use it. Like other services, the client name is simply the service name, `designate`. It uses the same, consistent authentication means as other CLI clients. It also provides quotas on the number of entities you can create.

```
$ designate quota-get tenant-id
+--------------------+-------+
| Field              | Value |
+--------------------+-------+
| domains            | 10    |
| domain_recordsets  | 500   |
| recordset_records  | 20    |
| domain_records     | 500   |
+--------------------+-------+
$
```

The `domains` entry is just what you might expect — it refers to domain names such as `example.com`. Most likely, you will be restricted to creating sub-domains of your organization's domain (e.g., `foo.example.com` or `foobar.example.com`). To understand the entries in this quota list, you need to know a little more about DNS.

> ### FULLY QUALIFIED DOMAIN NAMES
>
> Designate requires you to use fully qualified domain names—this includes the trailing ".". Strictly speaking, a name is not a FQDN without that, and Designate will enforce this.

For each domain, the DNS server holds *records*. Each record has a type, a name, a time-to-live and any associated data. While there are many record types, Designate supports nine common types as of the Kilo release, shown in the following table. Remember, each record also has a name—the example data shown here is the result of a query for that name.

RECORD TYPE	EXAMPLE DATA	DESCRIPTION
A	10.0.0.1	An IPv4 Address record.
AAAA	2001:DB8::1	An IPv6 Address record.
CNAME	foo.example. com.	A canonical name—this is an entry used to map one name to another. For example, if there is a DNS A record named bar.example.com, referring to 10.0.0.1, then you can create a CNAME record named foo.example.com. referring to bar. example.com. (the true, or canonical, name of the resource).
MX	10 mail.example .com.	A mail exchange server for the domain. This is used by mail agents to decide how to send mail to email addresses in this domain.
NS	ns1.example. com.	A name server record. The NS records on a domain specify which name servers are authoritative for the domain.
SSHFP	1 2 a4b1a288... 8821ab33ef	A public SSH host key fingerprint. This can be used to help verify hosts are who they say when using ssh.
SPF	v=spf1 ip4:192.0.2.0/24 a –all	A Sender Policy Framework record, used to help prevent email spoofing. It enables you to specify rules to filter out incoming email. TXT records are often used for this instead.
SRV	20 5 5060 sip. example.com.	A general service locator record. This is used to locate newer services rather than using a service-specific type like MX. See RFC 2782.
TXT	Some example text.	Arbitrary text, either for human or machine consumption.

Most often, you will use the A, AAAA, CNAME and perhaps MX records. For deploying some applications you may also take advantage of SRV records to advertise the availability of the application service to the rest of the organization. The remainder are primarily used by the administrator or for special purposes.

Record sets are groups of records with the same type, name, and TTL, but with different data. So, you can define an A record set with multiple IP addresses as data. The name is what you are actually using when you lookup a resource. For example, to lookup the address (A) record name `blue.foobar. example.com` from the DNS server at 172.16.98.136, you can use the `host` utility in Linux:

```
$ host -t A blue.foobar.example.com. 172.16.98.136
Using domain server:
Name: 172.16.98.136
Address: 172.16.98.136#53
Aliases:

blue.foobar.example.com has address 10.1.0.100
$
```

In the quota list, the `domain_recordsets` entry indicates the maximum number of record sets (ie, unique type/name combinations) you may have in a single domain. The `recordset_records` indicates the maximum number of records in a single record set. And finally the `domain_records` entry puts an additional constraint on total records in a domain.

Creating a domain using the CLI is straightforward—you use the `domain-create` command.

```
$ designate domain-create --ttl 3600 --name foobar.example.com. ↵
  --email info@example.com
+-------------+---------------------------------------+
| Field       | Value                                 |
+-------------+---------------------------------------+
| description | None                                  |
| created_at  | 2015-08-10T19:11:22.000000            |
| updated_at  | None                                  |
| email       | info@example.com                      |
| ttl         | 3600                                  |
| serial      | 1439233882                            |
| id          | 7254c2b3-187c-428e-974d-03bac08cb2af  |
| name        | foobar.example.com.                   |
+-------------+---------------------------------------+
$
```

You will notice that you must specify an email address as the contact for the domain. You also may specify the TTL value. This value is used by downstream caching name servers to know how long to hold on to the data before refreshing their cache. The value is in seconds; the longer you specify, the more time it will take for changes to go into effect across the entire Internet. However, specifying too low of a value for a frequently looked up domain can overburden your DNS servers. The default value in Designate is 3600, or one hour.

Once you have created a domain, you can start creating records. When you spin up a new VM, you can create a DNS entry for it so that other VMs within the cloud can access it by name, rather than by IP address. To create the record we used in the example lookup earlier, use this command.

```
$ designate record-create --type A --name blue.foobar.example.com. \
                    --data 10.1.0.100 foobar.example.com.
+-------------+---------------------------------------+
| Field       | Value                                 |
+-------------+---------------------------------------+
| description | None                                  |
| type        | A                                     |
| created_at  | 2015-08-10T19:18:59.000000            |
| updated_at  | None                                  |
| domain_id   | 7254c2b3-187c-428e-974d-03bac08cb2af  |
| priority    | None                                  |
| ttl         | None                                  |
| data        | 10.1.0.100                            |
| id          | fc83692a-f484-41fa-81c8-25300a908f7b  |
| name        | blue.foobar.example.com.              |
+-------------+---------------------------------------+
$
```

You will notice that the statement above says "within the cloud." The VM IP address at spin up is typically a private address, so machines external to the cloud will not be able to access the address directly. To enable external systems to access the VM via the name lookup, you need to associate a DNS entry with the floating IP address, not the private IP address.

One option to handle this cleanly is to use two different domain names for internal and external references. For example, if you want others in your organization to access your application from outside the cloud, you could create a domain `cloud.example.com` and another `cloud-local.example.com`. When you provision a VM (or a port in Neutron), you create an entry in the `cloud-local.example.com` domain. When you associate a floating IP address with that VM, you create a separate entry for the floating IP in `cloud.example.com`. Your internal cloud applications can refer to the `cloud-local.example.com` domain and the external clients to the `cloud.example.com` domain.

This works, but it's a pretty cumbersome solution. The alternative typically used in DNS is called split-horizon DNS. In this configuration, the DNS server can look at information about the inbound request, such as the DNS server IP address it came in through, or the source IP address of the query. It uses this information to choose the *DNS view* in which to evaluate the query response. DNS views enable you to define a different response for the same query—one in each view. So, you can define an A record for `www.cloud.example.com`. In the internal view that resolves to 10.1.0.100, and an A record for `www.cloud.example.com` in the external view that resolves to the floating IP address.

Unfortunately, as of the Kilo release, Designate does not yet support split-horizon DNS. However, it is on the roadmap so we can look forward to it in a future release.

Designate is a powerful and important part in automating your deployments. The ability to make your application immediately accessible via a DNS entry is critical to the rapid spin up of applications. Without the capabilities of Designate, application deployments in OpenStack would be limited by the often manual DNS entry creation process.

MAGNUM

One of the newest and most interesting components in the OpenStack ecosystem is a container focused project called Magnum. If you are unfamiliar with them, containers are a virtualization technology similar to virtual machines, only they work without a hypervisor. A more detailed conversation about exactly what containers are, how they compare to virtual machines, and the challenges/ solutions they provide can be found at the beginning of Chapter 6. In truth, when used in an OpenStack environment, containers actually have to live on top of classically provisioned instances. However, for the purposes of understanding what Magnum is and why it is important, containers can simply be looked at as another type of virtual machine that cannot be managed via Nova or Neutron.

Containers As A Service

Magnum is generally defined as a service that provides containers and container management within OpenStack. It allows you to programmatically provision, delete, and network containers without having to rely on a specific vendor, and does so in a multi-tenant capable manner.

There are currently a number of these vendor specific container orchestration systems. Google's Kubernetes, and Docker's Swarm are the most well known, and are both supported by Magnum. More recent offerings like Mesos and others are not yet supported, but are likely to be implemented at some point in the near future. One of the major concepts behind Mangum though, is that you don't have to rely on any specific vendor. Instead, OpenStack provides a set of agnostic APIs and interfaces that allow you to choose your own container type and orchestration system. This prevents vendor lock-in and allows you to more easily adopt new technology as it comes along.

Its ability to manage containers in a multi-tenancy fashion means that Magnum's functionality can be extended to consumers within an OpenStack-backed public cloud. Until now, in addition to being vendor specific, all of the prevailing solutions for container management would provide anyone with access to the orchestration layer, access to every container within it. With Magnum, containers are isolated by tenant, and their access is backed by Keystone.

Built Using Flannel, Kubernetes, and Docker?

Magnum is created from of a number of different components, but you will often hear that it is built upon three rather enigmatic technologies: flannel, Kubernetes, and Docker. It is helpful to know what each of these things are, but as you will see, it's a bit of a misnomer to consider Magnum as simply a combination of these things.

The first of these technologies, flannel (yes it's a lowercase f), was created by the people at CoreOS Inc. It is a virtual network that gives a subnet to each host for use with container runtimes. It provides a network binding between the classically provisioned host server and the multiple containers that exist on top of it, allowing traffic to be routed to and from specific containers. flannel is transparent in Magnum. There are no flannel APIs to speak to, nor is there any specific flannel functionality that has been exposed. Rather, flannel simply provides the networking to containers that Neutron could not.

The next one, Kubernetes, is a Google-backed open source project that provides Magnum with a driver for the orchestration of Docker containers. Like flannel, you don't interact directly with Kubernetes. Instead, you interact with the Magnum API, which can then use Kubernetes to provision, alter, or remove containers, pods and bays. Unlike flannel, by using alternate drivers such as Swarm or Mesos, it is possible to actually use Magnum without Kubernetes at all.

Lastly, there is Docker. Docker is the technology you have most likely heard of, but it can also be the most confusing since it is a number of different things. When people refer to Docker, they can be referring to it as a company. Docker actually offers a number of products centered around containers including Docker Hub (a hosted registry service) and Docker Swarm (mentioned earlier as an alternative to Kubernetes). The Docker Engine is also often referred to as just Docker. The Docker Engine is a runtime as well as a number of tools that allow you to build and run Docker containers.

In the case of OpenStack Magnum, Docker is basically a container format or software to run this format of containers on a host when using Swarm, which is an orchestration driver for these Docker formatted containers. While not supported currently, it is also possible that other container formats like Rocket could allow you to use Magnum without Docker at all.

The reference to these technologies as the basis for Magnum is not deceptive. It's meant to explain Magnum in its most common use case. Any reference on how to use Magnum will likely demonstrate how to deploy Docker containers using Kubernetes and flannel will back the networking behind the scenes. In truth though, they are simply more technology in an array of technical options that OpenStack and Magnum provide in a simplified way to use.

Built Using OpenStack

In addition to using Keystone for authentication and permissions, Magnum is actually built using a number of the other OpenStack projects that have already been discussed. It employs Heat for creating pods and bays where containers can live, Nova as its compute backbone, and Neutron to handle networking outside of the containers themselves. This can provide you with a lot of flexibility on exactly how containers are implemented in your environment.

For example, the computational unit that runs a cluster of containers (or node) can be anything that Nova can supply as a server. This means containers can be provisioned on top of bare metal severs or virtual machines. So not only does Magnum provide vendor agnostic containers, but it can be backed by vendor agnostic computing. The same can be said for its networking and even storage components. This is intentional, and is a great illustration of how OpenStack allows you to work with whatever assets you have available.

Building on top of the existing tools within OpenStack provides familiar interfaces, but that is not to say that using Magnum is no different than provisioning a VM and throwing it on a private network. The specific needs of containers that made them a poor fit for Nova, also make their orchestration and configuration a slightly different process.

Bay, Pods, Nodes, and Containers

As mentioned before, all containers that are part of Magnum run on top of Nova provisioned servers. What wasn't mentioned, was that these containers actually run on top of something called Bays that actually provides the container orchestration itself. Depending on the driver/vendor, containers or pods are then created on top of these bays in groups called nodes. Figure 3-11 may make this a little clearer.

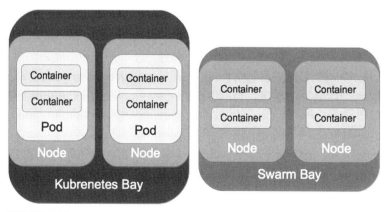

FIGURE 3-11

To provision a container, you must first select and provision a bay type. This will normally be done using one of several bay models that can be self-defined, but will most likely be provided by the system natively. Bay models are similar to Flavors when dealing with virtual machines. There will likely be one bay model available for each vendor/driver that has been configured in the system, and like most assets within OpenStack the bay models can be listed with a command. However, for now, selecting a bay model essentially means choosing between Kubernetes and Swarm.

Whatever the choice, the bay model is specified within a heat template and the actual bay is created through Heat. Bays are then available as stacks within the heat API or in the Horizon interface.

From this point, the Magnum API takes over. Within a bay you can call the magnum API to create containers (or pods), stop, start and reboot them like you can with VM's in Nova. This covers the basics, so you should have some idea of what Magnum is and how it works.

Magnum as the Future of OpenStack

There have been a lot of questions in the container community lately as to the need for OpenStack in the face of projects such as Kubernetes. After all, Kubernetes and Docker both provide nearly complete orchestration solutions.

A few reasons have already been mentioned as to why you might look toward OpenStack as a solution. Multi-tenancy and vendor agnostic APIs are both highly desirable qualities. Not having to acquire in-depth knowledge of some of the more esoteric technologies such as flannel can also be a big plus.

The big win here though is that OpenStack is trying to build a more future-proof platform and Magnum is likely to be a big part of OpenStack's future. Containers are excellent technology, but they are one of the fastest changing solutions out there. Like any new technology the initial winners are often long term losers, so it's risky to get in deep with any single container vendor/format/platform just yet. Because it is largely provider agnostic, placing a bet on Magnum is thus a much less risky venture. For example, the ability to shift gears from Kubernetes to Swarm without having to modify your deployment system could be a huge win, and while virtual machines are likely to be a big part of the landscape for many years to come, containers are here to stay.

MURANO: APPLICATION AS A SERVICE

From a cloud user perspective since OpenStack got its own orchestrator it made user experience more solid. It gave lots of improvements, but from cloud apps the integration process was too complicated due to specific limitations regarding the way Heat allows you to describe the infrastructure that needs to be deployed. So, even using the latest Heat HOT DSL cloud, consumers still can create a specific configuration, but writing a template would become a nightmare.

So, to improve user experience and provide more flexible capabilities for cloud users to deploy and maintain their own cloud-ready application it was decided to implement a new type of OpenStack service that would use Heat as the deployment tool that provides an API that will allow you to define applications using the same environment templates.

Application Catalog

Murano was designed to provide a way to make third-party applications and services running on VMs or even external services available as self-service for OpenStack. These applications may be a simple multi-tier application with auto-scaling and self-healing (within Heat capabilities). From the third-party tool developer's perspective, the application catalog will provide a way to publish applications, including deployment rules and requirements, suggested configurations, output parameters and billing rules. From the user's perspective, the application catalog will be a place to find and self-provision third-party applications and services, and integrate them into their environment, including billing costs.

The Application Catalog service was provided to simplify the process of creating applications and/or services on OpenStack. Installing third-party services and applications can be difficult in any environment, but the dynamic nature of an OpenStack environment can make this problem worse. Murano is designed to solve this problem by providing an additional integration layer between third party components and the OpenStack infrastructure. This integration layer makes it possible to provide both Infrastructure-as-a-Service and Platform-as-a-Service from a single control plane. For users, this control plan is a single interface from which you can provision an entire fully-functional cloud-based application environment. The Application Catalog service was integrated to all OpenStack components directly and indirectly via orchestrator (OpenStack Heat). The Ceilometer service collects usage information, which the Murano-API uses during billing rules processing to calculate billing information. The Murano API will expose API calls to manage (CRUD) services available for deployment. This API will be used by the Service administrator user interface to simplify service management.

Application Publisher

The process begins when an Application Publisher creates a new application description and publishes to the Application catalog. Once the application is uploaded then it'll be available within any application catalog instances, depending on the policies for that instance. Application Publishers should be able to create new applications by defining service metadata, describing properties and specifying all of the steps necessary for deploying the application and its dependencies. The developer can create this definition from scratch or use an existing definition by extending it, similar to inheritance in the object-oriented paradigm. The Application Publisher can define the external dependencies of an application. This list of dependencies defines the other services (specified by their type) that must be present in the environment when an application is being deployed.

The Application Publisher may define additional terms of use for an application. For example, the developer may limit its usage and extensibility (via inheritance or referencing from another application) or specify billing rules. Another important set of parameters that the Application Publisher may specify in the Service Definition are the usage metrics. These usage metrics define which aspects of the service should be monitored by Ceilometer or other monitoring tools supported by Murano when its instances are running. The Application Publisher can then specify the billing rules used with those metrics, essentially defining how much service usage will cost the user. A service definition is not bound to any particular OpenStack deployment or instance of Murano. The developer may create a service definition and then publish that definition in several service catalog instances.

Application Catalog Administrator

A published service/application definition is managed by the catalog administrator. Catalog administrators are the maintainers of the application service catalog. They have the ability to manually add or remove service definitions in a catalog, or act as moderators allowing or disallowing other Application Publishers to publish their service definitions. This control can be granular or not, as the administrator chooses. For example, the administrator may specify that any new submissions must be approved before being available to any end users, or the administrator may instead choose to make services available only to the OpenStack tenant associated with the application publisher until a service is approved.

Administrators may define their own billing rules, which will be in addition to the billing rules specified by the application publisher (if they were defined). This enables catalog administrators to cover the costs involved in running and maintaining the cloud.

Catalog administrators configures Role-Based Access Control rules (RBAC), which defines which users (which are associated with tenants) of the cloud have access to which services in the catalog, and whether they may be directly deployed or must be approved.

Application Catalog End Users

OpenStack users should be able to create environments composed of one or more available services. Application catalog consumptions by end users follows:

➤ The user browses a list of available services/applications and selects one or more for deployment. If a selected service has dependencies that require other services to be deployed in the same environment, the user may either select an instance of the necessary service from instances of that type that are already present in the environment, or add a new instance of that type instead. Dependencies may include other services, or they may include resources such as a floating IP address or license key. Each service added to the environment must be properly configured; the user is prompted to provide all required properties, and the input is validated according to the rules defined in each service definition. When the user has finished configuring the environment, he or she can deploy the environment—if he or she has the appropriate permissions. Deployment of the environment means that instances are created, services are deployed, and all required configuration actions take place and are accomplished properly.

➤ In some environments, it will be more appropriate for end users to submit their deployments to IT as a ticket. The IT department can then sanity-check the definitions, determine whether they are appropriate, and approve, modify, or reject the deployment. If the request is approved or modified, the IT department can then initiate the deployment, rather than the user.

➤ Users can browse any deployed environments for which they have permissions, and inspect their state. Inspection includes the ability to determine which services are running on which nodes, how the services are configured, and so on. Users can modify service settings, add new services or remove existing ones, validate the changes (i.e. check that all the required properties are set to valid values, all the service dependencies exist and so on), and redeploy the environment by propagating these changes into the Cloud. The user can also inspect the usage metrics of the services running in his or her environments, and see billable activities and the total amount of money spent for a particular service.

It sounds good when we're saying "an application" or "service," but we haven't defined what an application or service is, so it would be very useful to mention a few examples of an application that may be deploy within Murano:

➤ RDBS and NoSQL databases provided by Trove

➤ Hadoop Cluster provided by Sahara

➤ OpenShift PaaS Cluster provisioned through Heat

➤ MS SQL Cluster

➤ Chef Server or Puppet Master node installed my Murano workflows

➤ Nagios or Zabbix monitoring managed by Murano workflows

Murano Architecture

Following best practices in OpenStack, Murano was designed that way to have its components decoupled (see Figure 3-12), and it does consist of:

➤ murano-api, a RESTful service that faces to users

➤ murano-conductor, an actual engine that does most of heavy work for creating deployments

➤ murano-agent, a VM-side service that does software deployment and configuration according to a given application description

➤ backing service (MySQL)

➤ deployment engine (Heat)

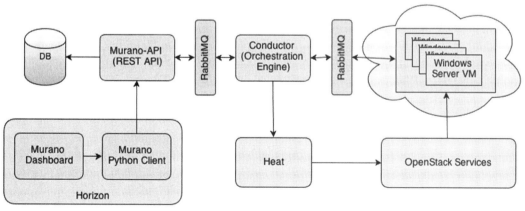

FIGURE 3-12

Murano Usage Example

Murano as an Application catalog intends to support applications, defined in different formats. One such example is Heat HOT DSL templates support. It means that any Heat template could be added as a separate application into the Application Catalog.

Before uploading an application into the catalog, it should be prepared and packaged appropriately. The Murano command line will do all of that preparation for you. Just choose the desired Heat Orchestration Template and perform the following command:

```
murano package-create  -template WordPress_2_Instances.yaml
```

Note that the Murano REST client allows you to specify additional parameters during package creation:

➤ application name

➤ application logo (used at UI)

➤ application description

➤ application author(s)

➤ output (local storage path to save created package)

➤ full name

But under the hood Murano does more than can be seen; it creates a manifest according to a given description, so in our case the manifest for given template would look something like this:

```
Format: Heat.HOT/1.0
Type: Application
FullName: io.murano.apps.linux.Wordpress
Name: Wordpress
Description: |
 WordPress is web software you can use to create a beautiful website or blog.
  This template installs a single-instance WordPress deployment using a local
  MySQL database to store the data.
Author: 'Openstack, Inc'
Tags: [Linux, connection]
Logo: logo.png
```

Once the manifest has been created, the user would need to package the application package before uploading it to Murano. Users must name the template file as `template.yaml`, and the name for the manifest file should be `manifest.yaml`. The user then needs to package an archive `*.zip` or `tar.gz` or whatever. You can do application importing:

```
murano package-import  -category Web -template wordpress.tar.gz
```

This is only a basic example of how users can consume Murano and its capabilities as an Application catalog for OpenStack. For other use cases and usage examples please take a look at `http://murano.readthedocs.org/`.

From a cloud users perspective Murano is very useful. Outside of the OpenStack ecosystem you should look at RedHat OpenShift, which is a PaaS platform for application deployment and management. You might also look at Gigaspaces Cloudify, which is a PaaS solution that aims to be a complete substitution for Heat, Murano, and Solum for OpenStack enterprise customers/consumers. But Murano is an official part of OpenStack, so it means that Murano is free and comes out of the box for any OpenStack distributions.

CEILOMETER: TELEMETRY AS A SERVICE

Applications and systems require monitoring. In order to ensure continuous service delivery, you need to know whether your applications or infrastructure running those applications have encountered any faults, and whether they are experiencing heavy utilization. Ceilometer is primarily focused on the latter function—monitoring resource utilization across the cloud, although it does provide some alarming and notification functionality as well. Ceilometer monitoring may be used for capacity planning, billing and chargeback, as well as elastic scaling.

Ceilometer Architecture

The major components of the Ceilometer architecture include the API, the polling agents, collectors for storing agent results, alarm evaluators, alarm notifiers, and possibly several different backend databases (see Figure 3-13).

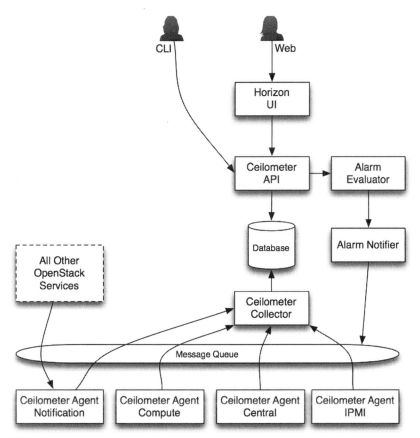

FIGURE 3-13

There are two basic types of Ceilometer agents: notification receivers and pollers. The polling agents periodically request various metrics from other services. For example, the `ceilometer-agent-compute` will run on a compute node and gather guest CPU statistics from the hypervisor on that compute node. The notification receiver agents simply listen on the message bus, and gather information about the inner workings of other OpenStack systems based on their notification outputs.

All of this data collected by the agents is sent back to the `ceilometer-collector`, which is a daemon (or many instances of the daemon) that transforms and stores the data into the backend databases. There may be several different databases used, based upon the different types of data.

The `ceilometer-alarm-evaluator` process is configured to look at the data in the system and evaluate whether alarming criteria are met. These criteria are user-defined and configurable. Once the criteria are met, then `ceilometer-alarm-notifier` will take an action based upon the raised alarm. This could be calling a specific URL, or another user-specified action.

Elastic Scaling with Ceilometer

In Chapter 6, you will see in detail how your applications can scale elastically by combining the telemetry data from Ceilometer with the orchestration capabilities of Heat. In short, you configure Heat and Ceilometer to monitor the Ceilometer metrics for a group of resources (say, VMs and you are monitoring CPU utilization). When a threshold is reached, an alarm fires, which in turn calls out to Heat to scale up (or down) the number of instances. This is a powerful way to meet uneven demand, while optimizing the costs associated with an application.

SUMMARY

There is a lot to be said about using OpenStack as simply a platform for provisioning servers and networks. In doing so, it would be easy to discount many of the projects discussed in this chapter. After all, most of us have made it this far without application packaging, containers, or any sort of orchestration system. However, the expanded ecosystem of technology presented here hints at a larger goal for OpenStack. It is trying to be more than just an IAAS provider. In fact, many of these projects offer solutions to the fundamental needs of web development. It's almost uncommon these days for an application not to involve a database (Trove), DNS entries (Designate), and alerts (Ceilometer). Even though it isn't scripted and labeled as orchestration, such applications also require manual configuration and deployment in some manner.

In this sense, OpenStack is attempting to make the process of developing and deploying cloud based applications not just possible, but easier and more formalized. It's also trying to provide scriptable self-service solutions for some of the more common tasks in web development in general. For that reason alone, these secondary components are worth learning about and experimenting with. So before we move on and start looking at what a cloud application looks like, take another look at this chapter and ask yourself if these projects provide solutions for problems you frequently encounter. In all likelihood, they do, and utilizing them can make you more productive, and your applications less proprietary.

PART II
Developing and Deploying Applications with OpenStack

Application Development

WHAT'S IN THIS CHAPTER?

➤ Legacy applications

➤ Why do you need migration to clouds?

➤ Migrate-to-cloud methodology

➤ Convert your application into an OpenStack app

➤ Building applications from scratch

➤ Development stack

➤ Application network connectivity

➤ Application security

➤ Hands-on application deployment

In this chapter you will be explicitly shown how to perform a legacy application migration from a self-maintained proprietary environment to an OpenStack environment. But before diving in, let's make sure we understand the full meaning of the term "legacy application." In computer science, legacy applications are those that come from platforms and techniques that exist earlier than the current technology stack, and in general these are applications that are serving critical business needs in an organization. Okay, let's get started.

CONVERTING A LEGACY APP TO AN OPENSTACK APP

When the word "legacy" appears within any context, the first thought is that we're talking about something very old that can't be adjusted to the current state of things. But if we're talking about software, a legacy application is not necessarily defined by age. Legacy may refer to the lack of vendor support or a system's incapacity to meet organizational requirements. Legacy conditions refer to a system's difficulty (or inability) to be maintained, supported or improved. A legacy application is usually incompatible with newly purchased systems. An organization might continue to use legacy applications for a wide range of reasons, such as the following:

➤ It works, so why should we invest more?

➤ The legacy system is complex, and documentation is poor. Simply its defining scope can be difficult.

➤ A redesign is costly, due to complexity or a monolithic architecture.

Why Migrate to Clouds?

In most cases, it is really complicated to keep apps running during updates without a maintenance window. In the case of legacy applications, "update" even means that the whole application was re-written using new programming languages, and involving new types of services (for example, switching from self-maintained databases to cloud databases). This should make legacy applications easier to maintain in the future, given that you can update applications without having to entirely rewrite them, which allows a company to use their applications on any environments or operating systems.

Yet, for the enterprise and their legacy applications, a system redesign would take a lot of effort (money, time, and an unclear value-add).

Enterprise IT organizations are facing critical challenges maintaining legacy applications:

➤ Cost of proprietary hardware and software

➤ Attrition in people with qualified skills and experience

➤ Inability to support the modern computing demands of mobile and big fast data

Cloud computing can help with legacy applications in terms of maintenance for the IT department. Unfortunately, many IT organizations see the prospect of modernizing legacy applications as a "mission impossible" with the path forward "too cloudy" and the costs and risks too great. They have a point, but there are some factors that can help determine if our legacy applications can migrate to the cloud:

➤ **Structure:** A large, single-tiered, monolithic legacy application isn't a good fit for clouds. Efficiencies are gained when the application is modular or the load can be spread out over several application instances to allow high availability (HA) and scalability.

➤ **Software and hardware dependencies:** A particular chip set or an external device such as an eye scanner might not be a good fit for the cloud. The same thing can apply to software, since a legacy application may require the use of a specific operating system or set of libraries that can't be used in a cloud nor be virtualized. If this is the case, then definitely an app like this is not a good fit for the cloud.

➤ **Durability and fault-tolerance:** Despite application Service Level Agreements (SLA), we're living in a world where everything breaks: networks are disrupted, servers fail, and the multi-tenant usage of an application looks like a Distributed Denial-of-Service attack (DDoS) instead of showing regular behavior. Applications must survive or be sturdy enough to contend with any given issues.

As a result, many enterprise companies are resigning themselves to live with legacy applications because moving to the cloud is not a step forward due to the amount of effort that is required. Eventually, the business loses confidence in IT's ability to deliver, and the costs continue to rise without corresponding value or any visible benefit. Let's examine some specific advantages for moving from a legacy app to a cloud app.

First, moving your legacy app to the cloud lowers the total cost of ownership. Maintaining mainframe license leasing costs is one area to look at. Since the cloud further commoditizes the infrastructure, modernizing mainframe apps to the cloud should decrease the total cost due to the absence of needing to maintain the environment by itself.

In clouds, flexibility defines the rate at which legacy application needs can be successfully adjusted to meet the ever-changing needs of the business. In the case of environment delivery, clouds come out on top compared to self-managed hardware. This is due to the flexibility of the cloud environment definition and the pace of provisioning as well.

From a business perspective it's always better to spend less and achieve more. In the case of clouds, hardware costs less because cloud consumers don't need to manage their hardware themselves, so they can avoid spending money for electricity and hardware upgrades.

In the case of proprietary hardware, to scale up you need to buy new hardware, set it up, and manage it. At the point when you must scale down, the organization will end up with unused hardware. With a cloud solution you can scale your operation and you don't need to buy hardware, all of which saves time.

Developers of course create the code that must be tested in the environment that is close to production. In the case of proprietary hardware it is necessary to have a dedicated development/testing environment maintained by the IT department, probably on one server. Developing in the cloud, however, only requires developers to have a separate account to work with and it is easy to create production-like environments to run new code and/or reproduce bugs.

These are all great reasons why you should consider moving from a legacy environment to a cloud environment, and the cloud does virtualize and orchestrate a lot of the manual jobs that are being performed by an IT department. These include processes such as networking, software installation, VM hardware customization, scaling, and more. And don't forget updating to a cloud-ready application can be the right business model for enterprise customers.

Migrate-To-Clouds Methodology

So, if your application is lucky enough to be a cloud-ready application, and it seems like you have convinced your company to move from self-maintained hardware to the cloud, it is important to understand the widely-applied strategies that you can use to switch to the cloud:

➤ **Lift and shift:** If your application environment can easily migrate from a legacy environment to the cloud then you just need to lift it and shift it to the cloud environment.

➤ **GreenField approach** (`http://www.thegreenfieldorganisation.com/approach2.html`): From the definition, you can see that this is risky. This approach of rewriting an entire legacy application is the most expensive and critical modernization approach. However, automated code analysis, code conversion, testing, and cloud deployment tools can greatly reduce the risks and costs associated with this. So, in this case it is strongly recommended that you figure out the true risk rate before implementing this approach.

➤ **Incremental replacement:** This approach requires you to replace the single unit of an application at a time. This has proven to be cost-effective and less risky. Unfortunately, there are no guidelines that can really help you since most every application is unique.

Consider all of the integrations between the legacy application infrastructure and other applications—integrating applications will need to be updated and tested taking into account the cloud capabilities. This is a very important step since it's necessary to implement deployment architecture. Once complete, you should define the hardware configuration for each application's component (clouds offer various types of business models: paying for resources on demand or paying for a year/month subscription).

You next thing to consider is accessibility. This step defines the networking configuration, exposing which components of an application should be accessible to other services. It is important to leave an application networking configuration in the same configuration that was applied before, so you end up with the expected behavior that was observed with the legacy application hardware.

For software configuration on cloud instances there are two steps: software installation (can be done on pre-provisioning or post-provisioning) and post-installation (post-provisioning) configuration. Cloud providers are offering base images with operating systems, but this is not what should be used, because of the availability of more advanced ways of software installation at the pre-provisioning stage. It is more than recommended to create custom images for VM provisioning, and for this task please take a look at `http://docs.openstack.org/developer/diskimage-builder/`. At this point we're ready to deploy the cloud-ready application and do post-provisioning software configuration to start the application.

The last step is to apply monitoring systems to track the environment state during its work. Here's the short list of what should be taken into account for this:

➤ Hardware configuration for application components

➤ Application components deployment strategy

➤ Networking configuration

➤ Custom image composing

➤ Environment deployment

➤ Post-provisioning software configuration

➤ Applying monitoring

➤ Testing an application

It doesn't seem like this list is complete, but if you combine it with the already pre-defined list of application dependencies you should be able to observe the full list of application needs. Once you have this full list, then you should begin the actual converting (in this case converting means applying a migration strategy to an application and doing the actual deployment) of the legacy application to a full-gear OpenStack application.

BUILDING APPS FROM SCRATCH

Not every application in the world is a legacy application because many of them were developed when clouds became popular and applications themselves were already hardware-agnostic, but not built for clouds at all. So it is possible that migrating to the cloud may not give the necessary value add expected by a cloud-oriented business model. And this means that creating a new application from scratch may give that benefit, but in a longer period of time.

Application Design Guidelines for OpenStack

Developing a new application that will go to the cloud requires specific guidelines when developing and integrating applications specifically to OpenStack:

➤ Be a pessimistic as possible. Everything breaks so, "love your chaos monkey" (a chaos monkey is a service that identifies groups of systems and randomly terminates one of the systems in a group).

➤ Put your eggs into multiple baskets. Leverage multiple regions, availability zones, and compute hosts. Design portability (remember lift and shift).

➤ Think of scalability.

➤ When integrating into OpenStack don't forget to be paranoid—design security wisely.

➤ Manage your data wisely. Data is always a critical resource, so don't hesitate to enable data replication/clustering, and do a regular backup.

➤ Be dynamic. Let your application be smart by enabling auto-scaling.

➤ Hands off—automate all business processes to increase consistency.

➤ Not all applications require the same high level of security.

➤ Predictability and elasticity—with increasing/decreasing amount of resources the application should act in a predictable way.

➤ Divide and conquer. Make your application granular as much as possible, especially when integrating HA solutions.

➤ Due to networking latency it is necessary to keep your data partitions close to each other but not on the same compute host or region.

➤ Loose coupling, service interfaces, separation of concerns, abstraction and well defined APIs deliver flexibility.

➤ Be cost aware: autoscaling, data transmission, virtual software licenses, reserved instances, and so on can rapidly increase monthly usage charges. Monitor usage closely.

Best Practices in Cloud-Ready App Development

If your application is divided into a server and client side you need to consider if it is necessary to consume the OpenStack API (managing cloud resources). You must decide if you want to use existing client bindings for OpenStack services or implement your own. For example, if you are reusing existing ones, it is recommended that you use Python, because the OpenStack community does development and delivery for client bindings for you. If you don't use Python, you will have to research if there are supported up-to-date client bindings or you must implement your own. So it is up to your development team to decide which language should be used for development, including all given points (ability to code fast, work on virtualized hosts, etc.).

Once you have made a decision regarding base development technologies (including coding language, additional software, SDKs, etc.) it is time to figure out your best practices for application development.

Manage Your Code Appropriately

Applications that are being developed should be version-controlled using any software such as GIT, Mercurial, or SVN. It is very important if the application is distributed that each of its components should be treated as separate cloud applications. Note that multiple applications that are sharing the same codebase is a violation of this methodology. So, basically, keep your applications separate. Going back to the version control system, it is more than obvious to use them because there would be a need to have, for example, a stable production version or staging that is being recently developed.

Dependency Management

For any cloud-ready applications it is necessary that you explicitly define their dependencies in a manner that is understandable to the packaging system of the distribution. A golden rule is to never rely on a deployment environment, since it is possible that from version to version there are some packages that might not be presented, which means explicit is better than implicit. A simple example is how Ubuntu 12.04 has PostgreSQL 9.1 in its source repositories, but Ubuntu 14.XX doesn't.

Configuration Management

Make your application configurable. It is possible that the deployment environment may vary (deployment host name, credentials, IP addresses in case of Switches, NATs, etc.). There are also application configuration parameters that are remaining the same across deployments, so it doesn't mean they should not be configurable, but use some sort of default values. Another important item to take advantage of is configuration parameter grouping. For example, if an application uses a database and an AMQP service for its internal needs, please put those options into different sections such as [database],[messaging], and for different types of deployments it would be nice to have sections like [production], [staging], if necessary.

Build, Release, and Have Fun

There are four main stages before allowing access to an application:

➤ **Build:** Simple, right? Make a distribution of your source code, and it doesn't matter what it will be: DEB, RPM, Python EGG, GitHub Tag, or whatever.

➤ **Staging:** Often takes a couple iterations. In the real world, a staging environment with an installed build is being examined using post-deployment verifications. By saying "post-deployment" verification we mean that the QA team runs a set of scenarios that mimic user behavior. During staging it is possible to discover certain bugs or unexpected application behavior. In this case the QA team prepares an additional set of test scenarios for new staging deployment.

➤ **Release:** The Kraken! Often the release stage involves new version publishing, so prepare version release documentation, and do any announcements within any available communication channels. Before doing a release it is necessary to prepare a mechanism for the user reports (JIRA, Slack channel, or a mailing list).

➤ **Have fun:** Yes, have fun with user reports, issues, and new requested version features.

Prepare Your App to Work at Scale or Die

Most distributed applications are distributed because keeping a single instance of an application gives a zero fault-tolerance. But let's figure out how an application can scale without consuming more VMs. Almost all development frameworks have multithreaded, processed libraries for creating a services like RESTful services or application engines that can handle multiple requests at the same time. The term "worker" is an entity that is being managed by a task broker. Here's a simple example: the Python library Flask supports processes and threads, but because of its implementation it is not recommended to use it as a user accessible service. In production it is recommended to use Nginx + Python Gunicorn + Flask, but let's understand why. Nginx works as a proxy and it does a good job, but Python Gunicorn works as a local RESTful service wrapper and allows you to run an application within multiple workers that are being executed as separate processes with a common task distributor. The Flask application holds an implementation of the RESTful application.

Speaking of the number of workers, take into account that it's strongly suggested to run only one type services per VM instance. So, your application should run a number of workers equal to the number of vCPU. However, we are still talking about a single VM with multiple workers in it, and we still at the point where we are, an application should survive and be available for its users. And here comes load balancing and high availability—cloud-ready applications should be ready to work correctly within multiple instances behind a load balancer (each application doesn't store data locally, but does persist into a backing service) within an HA mode.

Why is high availability and load balancing needed? First of all, HA mode gives you the ability to access applications within its multiple instances (example, Galera master-2-muster replication), so you have an instance for an A to Z user who can get the same data from any of them. This is how HA mode works. But in developing an application that is consuming a cloud application, it is not very useful to remember a set of IP addresses or domain names for each application instance. Load balancing provides you with the ability to hide the cloud application behind one IP address or DNS name. This is beneficial because the load balancer distributes requests between cloud application instances. Because of this, your application should not have to worry about accessibility of a specific instance.

Maximize Robustness with Fast Bootstrapping and Graceful Shutdown

OpenStack applications should strive to minimize bootstrap time. In an ideal world, an application takes a few seconds from the bootstrap execution until the process is up and ready to receive tasks. A short startup time provides more agility for the release process and scaling up; and it helps to improve robustness, because the application instance manager can more easily move it to new physical machines (by auto-scaling events). Applications shut down gracefully when they receive a SIGTERM signal from their manager. Unfortunately most application developers are putting worries about a graceful shutdown to the backlog.

Keep Development, Staging, Pre-Production and Production As Close As Possible

As developers you need to keep in mind the following:

➤   Make your time gap small between writing code and putting it into staging/pre-production/production.

➤   Make the personnel gap small. You are the committer of new code, so you are responsible for deployment within any environment.

➤   Make the tools gap small. Each developer should keep their environment almost similar to a production environment.

Keep this in mind when testing your code. As a developer you should resist the urge to use different backing services between development and production, even when adapters theoretically abstract away any differences in backing services. Differences between backing services means that tiny incompatibilities crop up, causing code that worked and passed any types of tests in development or staging to fail in production.

Test As Much As Possible

In application development that involves the use of attached resources it is necessary to write the next types of testing:

➤   **Fake-mode integration tests:** This type of testing allows you to examine your code not involving attached resources (for on-demand services that cost you money) but use instead their fake implementation stubs.

➤   **Real-mode tests:** Handle any API backing services.

➤   **Post-deployment checks:** This type examines user stories, scenarios against deployed application, and often takes part at staging and pre-production.

Continuous Integration/Continuous Delivery

Continuous Integration (CI) is the practice of testing each change done to your codebase automatically and as early as possible. So, for the sake of stability insurance, your project should use CI votes as part of code review, because CI would prevent you from merging code that doesn't work correctly. Continuous Delivery (CD) follows your tests results to push your changes to either a staging or pre-production (pushing into production may cause problems). In any case, CD makes sure a version of your code is always accessible. It is possible that you need to keep your own CI/CD due to specific reasons. But if your organization is small and you don't have enough resources to invest into building your own environment, you can use any CI-as-a-Service. There are two well-known services: Travis CI (`https://travis-ci.org/`) and Circle CI (`https://circleci.com/`). Feel free to pick the one you like.

So, you have SDKs, and you have guidelines on how to do this, and how not to. You have CI and CD. It is now time to do some tricky magic—deploy an application, a real cloud application.

OPENSTACK APP DESCRIPTION AND DEPLOYMENT STRATEGIES

So, this is a good time to talk a bit about legacy application description.

Coming back to the methodology of migrating an application to the cloud, you need to have all of the steps implemented that we have covered in this chapter for your application to become cloud-ready. Let's assume that you have these inputs:

➤   Application consists of these components: Web UI, RESTful service, back-end service, and a backing service.

➤   Web UI and RESTful service are facing to users.

➤   Back-end service is accessible only by a RESTful service.

➤   Backing service can be an attached service or it can be the part of an application. Only application back-end services talk to the backing service.

So, what would be the best solution to make this application cloud-ready?

DEMO APPLICATION SOURCE CODE

You can access the source code from our demo application via GitHub: `https://github.com/johnbelamaric/openstack-appdev-book`.

Cloud-Ready App Description

Following the migration steps, you need to decouple your legacy application into multiple nodes. Let's assume that your application consists of these nodes (see Figure 4-1):

➤   Web UI node

➤   RESTful service node

➤ Back-end service node

➤ Backing service (MySQL)

You need to define the hardware requirements, i.e. in terms of OpenStack – define specific instance flavors that describe the number of vCPUs, RAM, ephemeral and root disk. For the sake of simplicity let's assume that you are ok with only one flavor, but most real-world cases must define flavor parameters for each application service, because of the workflows. In most cases, some instances would require a lot of vCPUs to do calculations, and other instances would require tons of RAM and a root disk to do data processing (Hadoop and its HDFS with map-reduce would be a good example here).

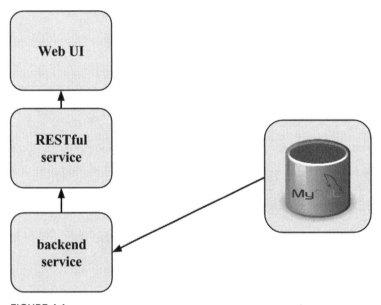

FIGURE 4-1

For the cursory glance it looks fine. Users are able to access the application within the Web UI or RESTful service. Such an application would be a good example of how to integrate into the cloud since that given app is multi-tiered.

When we're talking about MySQL and backing services in general we have to consider that this type of service should be durable, and available no matter what happens. So, based on given inputs we need to figure out which operating system is needed, how much resources (RAM, vCPU are needed), and do we want to keep MySQL data as an attached block storage provided by Glance (these steps and decisions are very important, because all of this affects the lifecycle of the service). So, relying on background knowledge we strongly recommend you use a flavor that does have at least 4 vCPUs and at the very least 8GB RAM. Regarding storage, we recommend you use a block storage volume to allow for quick fail recovery and consistency.

The application components are the Web UI, RESTful service, and back-end service nodes. By itself the RESTful service node is not a standalone application that is being deployed as part of application delivery. According to best practices of application development, it should be treated as a separate application. Coming back to what we've discussed for MySQL, we need to figure out what would be the best options for deploying this application. By itself, the RESTful service is a stateless application, but it has to work fast to serve multiple users at the same time. It is recommended that you use a flavor that has lots of RAM, a vCPU question is not critical for now, and we don't need block storage for now because there's nothing to store, because we just process the requests. Speaking of an application back-end service, this part of the application is tough, since it does almost all of the heavy work. So this node should be very powerful, and it has to have lots of vCPUs, RAM, and disk space that are required by an application's workflow definition (not block storage, but flavor root disk). There is nothing different about the Web UI node—it should be fast, and there are no other demands.

Once the RESTful service and Web UI nodes get deployed, users will be able to access the RESTful service within the RESTful service node by its IP address and Web UI independently (according to a given schema, UI can work with single instance of a RESTful service at the same time). Please keep in mind that in the real world, each service that is facing to a user needs must be solid and ready to be stress-tested, because in some cases users are acting like DDoS attackers.

After completing this section we have a cloud-based application that has been deployed, taking into account all best practices and application demands.

Network Deployment Strategy

Let's go back and describe the application deployment schema. We have three types of services, in other words three different cloud applications, and each application deserves its own access level from the outside. For example, the current schema describes an application deployment within a single network that seems ok for an example, but such SLA doesn't look good for other cases. Web UI and RESTful services are facing to users within a public network, so the user can access both of them and such things break the concepts of a secure SLA.

Public and Private (Management) Network

You might suggest that each component use its own network, but it will add an overhead since you'd need to do routing and might eventually end up with complex, hardly maintainable solution. Of course you are not trying to link multiple datacenters into a single network for this solution. In this case it would be enough to define two networks—public (with Internet, and accessible from the outside) and private (no Internet, and accessible from a public network). First of all, it is necessary to figure out which network each service belongs to. It's easy with our example: network placement is described in Figure 4-2; Web UI as public NIC in Figure 4-3; RESTful services as private NIC in Figure 4-4; application back-end service as private NICs in Figure 4-5; and MySQL node as private NIC in Figure 4-6.

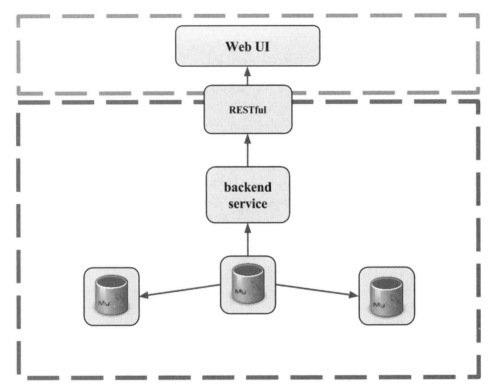

FIGURE 4-2

As you can see, based upon the description given above, application tiers may have a couple of networks attached to prevent unwanted access. Now, let's take a look at each component, starting with the Web UI. Since this type of application tier needs to be available to users it should have a public IP address and it doesn't have internal network access to prevent security risks. So, the green color wire corresponds to the public network shown in Figure 4-3.

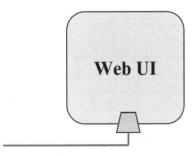

FIGURE 4-3

The RESTful service tier is similar to the Web UI tier for this application, since the component should be accessible within the public IP address. But, since these components are tied to the back-end service, it has to have access to the private network (see Figure 4-4). The red line wire corresponds to the private network access.

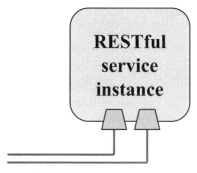

FIGURE 4-4

Going forward, let's examine the application back-end service tier and its networking, shown in Figure 4-5. This part of the application is only accessible within the private network.

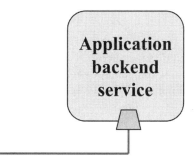

FIGURE 4-5

Take a look at the last component of our application—MySQL (see Figure 4-6). This part of the application follows a similar networking strategy as the back-end service. The private network and this component are accessible only by the back-end service.

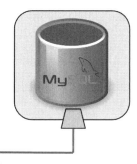

FIGURE 4-6

Keep in mind that the accessibility of the application component and the network strategy requires an SLA setup for an application within given networks. In the case of OpenStack it is recommended that you use security groups (available in Nova-network and Neutron):

➤ **For the Web UI instance:** Suppose we use Nginx for hosting the UI code and default ports for HTTP and HTTPS. It would be necessary to close any ports except 80 and 443 for inbound connections and open the port for the load balancer for outbound connections.

➤ **For RESTful service nodes:** Security groups for inbound connections require a load balancer port only. Security groups for outbound connections require AMQP broker ports or direct access ports to the application back-end service.

➤ **For the application back-end service:** Security groups for inbound connections require a RESTful service for nodes ports from their IPs only or no rules (in the case of AMQP transport, there would be only outbound connections to the AMQP broker). Security groups for outbound connections require MySQL ports with a MySQL master instance IP as CIDR, and in the case of AMQP, broker instance(s) port(s).

➤ **For MySQL node:** Security groups for inbound connections require an application back-end service port, and MySQL slave ports with their IPs as CIDRs. Security groups for outbound connections require a master node port and an IP as CIDR.

SUMMARY

In this chapter we covered how to do a migration, including limitations and critical points, but it wasn't just a simple lift and shift. We tried to explicitly explain how to decouple application services, and how to implement a deployment strategy, including networking and SLA. We've amended steps like application testing and software configuration, due to the variety of techniques applicable for such cases, and also we've skipped monitoring because of the complexity of trying to describe the generic use case for cloud application monitoring. But every other case and technique described in this chapter are applicable for any types of cloud-ready applications, regardless if they are a legacy application in the past or a completely new application that is under design right now.

5

Improving on the Application

WHAT'S IN THIS CHAPTER?

➤ Understanding the types of failure scenarios that can affect applications running in the cloud

➤ Providing access into the application and understanding how hostname and IP addresses play an important role

➤ Methods for scaling an application to multiple instances and regions and adapting to events in the environment

➤ Improving the basic application

It is common for applications to be initially developed for the cloud in a very simple manner. The developer may start with deploying the application as a single instance in the cloud. If the application has different types of functions, such as a web front-end and a database back-end, these functions can be broken into a couple different instances.

This chapter discusses what you as the developer need to do next. You need to know what kind of failures occur in the cloud and how those failures could affect the application. You also need to understand the application components and how they relate to failures in order to build a more robust and reliable application.

Different techniques are examined on how to scale the application in the cloud. The chapter also takes a look at performance and why it is important to know when and where performance issues occur. Often, scaling the application in the right places can mitigate performance issues when they occur.

The chapter also takes a look at data protection. How important is the data to the application? Is it important that data is never lost? Can some data be lost and recreated or replaced later? How important is the data? The answers to these questions can affect decisions on how data is protected in the cloud.

High availability means that the application is always available and minimizes downtime. It also means that the application should run reliably and be performant. This chapter takes a look at what it means to build a highly available application and some of the challenges developers may run into along the way.

Finally, we take a basic application and improve upon it to demonstrate the concepts in this chapter. Three different components are examined as they are taken to the next level in providing high availability.

> **DEMO APPLICATION SOURCE CODE**
>
> You can access the source code from our demo application via GitHub: `https://github.com/johnbelamaric/openstack-appdev-book`.

FAILURE SCENARIOS

Operators of the OpenStack cloud understand that it is difficult to keep the cloud running problem-free. The larger a cloud environment is, the more likely problems will occur. Developers need to understand what types of problems can affect the application and how to deal with them. Applications that take these failure scenarios into account will suffer less downtime and continue to run, even when problems do occur.

Hardware Failure

A typical OpenStack environment contains a few administrative servers to help run the cloud, as well as a bunch of other servers, called compute nodes, that provide the means for applications to be deployed to the cloud. The bigger the environment, the more hardware that will be required to run it.

Eventually, a server's hardware is going to fail. The most common types of hardware failure include disk drives, memory, CPU, power supplies, and network interfaces. Some hardware failures can bring the server down entirely. Some hardware failures may result in a reduced server performance. Other failures may not affect the server at all, such as one of the power supplies failing.

If an application is built without high availability in mind, it is likely that the application has many single points of failure built into it. If a server fails and any one of those single points of failures is on that server, the application will fail as well.

Network Failure

There are several different ways that a network can be setup and operated within an OpenStack environment. However, from the perspective of the instance running in the cloud, it has a network interface card with an active network link and an assigned IP address. All that matters to the instances is that it is connected to the network and that it can access other instances or devices on the network reliably.

One way that instances experience network failures is when something breaks in the OpenStack network stack. The instance still sees a network and still has an IP address, but it is unable to connect to any other devices on the network and other devices are unable to connect to the instance. The root cause of the network issue will affect how network connectivity is restored in the instance. For example, issues with Neutron or OVS on the compute node where the instance exists may require the instance to be rebooted in order to restore connectivity.

Another way that instances experience network failures is through the loss of the IP address on its network interface card. The IP address is provided to the instance by a DHCP service that runs on the network node. It is rare for the DHCP service itself to go down, but issues in the OpenStack network stack may disrupt the ability for the DHCP service to communicate to the instance. Default configurations of OpenStack tend to expire DHCP leases very quickly, which results in the instance renewing its DHCP lease often. Network communication issues can disrupt the renewal process, which results in the IP address being released from the instance and ultimately taking its network down.

The operating system installed on the instance can make a difference on how it responds to network issues as well. For example, when an instance loses a DHCP address, Ubuntu typically continues to retry renewing the DHCP address. When the network issues are resolved, the renewal process succeeds and the IP address is restored. However, RedHat and CentOS are commonly configured by default to give up after the renewal process fails, which means that even if the network issues are resolved, the instance is no longer attempting to renew the DHCP lease and permanently stays off the network. The easiest way to resolve the network connectivity issue with the instance is to reboot the instance. A better solution would be to adjust the DHCP client for RedHat and CentOS instances to always retry DHCP renewals instead of giving up.

External network issues can also occur. A typical OpenStack environment will be set up with a set of administrative nodes, numerous compute nodes, one or more switches to connect all the nodes together, and a router for the switches to connect to for traffic coming in or leaving the OpenStack environment. The switches are critical to the operation of the environment, as that is the lifeline between the compute node and the network node. A switch problem can disrupt communication between the nodes. An issue at the router may not disrupt communication between nodes, but it may prevent access to other things on the network, such as DNS lookups, access to authentication servers, and any other network services the instances may depend on.

Storage Failure

An OpenStack instance makes use of either ephemeral storage or persistent storage, or even a combination of both. Ephemeral storage is defined as storage that may not be permanent. For example, the storage associated with the instance could be deleted if the instance itself is terminated. Persistent storage is defined as storage that is permanent. If an instance is terminated, the persistent storage associated with the instance is typically not deleted, but may be detached and made available to be attached to another instance.

Persistent storage is typically implemented as object storage or block storage. Object storage is often implemented using Swift or some other product that implements the Swift API, such as Ceph. When using object storage, containers are created and binary objects are stored inside the containers.

Instances can retrieve the stored objects using the API implemented by the object storage system. Block storage shows up to instances as block devices in the operating system, which can then be mounted on a directory or used as a raw device.

Ephemeral storage is similar to block storage in the way that it appears to the instance as block devices. This means that instances can mount the block device on a directory or use it as a raw device. Ephemeral is configured by default in OpenStack to use the storage from the disks in the compute nodes. It is possible to configure ephemeral storage using other architectures too, but using compute node disks for ephemeral storage is the most common usage. Unless an instance is launched using a "boot from volume" method, the instance will be created using the compute node ephemeral storage.

One of the most common hardware failures encountered in an OpenStack environment is disk failure. Disk failures can have a wide effect on instances, depending on how OpenStack is configured and how the disk failure affects the device it is installed in. Ephemeral storage will likely have a greater effect on instances than persistent storage. With ephemeral storage, data is very unlikely to be replicated and the chance for data loss will be higher. For persistent storage, data is often replicated and can be accessed in multiple ways. If a single disk fails in a persistent storage cluster, the instance may not even notice, since the data remains available and consistent.

Let's look at the case where the instance is running on ephemeral storage. The operating system is on an ephemeral root disk that lives on a compute node. The compute node could be configured with some kind of RAID that replicates data behind the scenes. A single disk failure may not affect the instance at all, much like a single disk failure in persistent storage. However, it is not uncommon to see a RAID device experience a disk failure that results in the block device going into read-only mode inside the instance. Even though the data is still available and can be read by the instance, writes are blocked. Read-only mode usually occurs at the compute node level, which affects all the instances running on that node. Rebooting the compute node is often needed to fix the issue.

If the compute node is not configured with RAID or some kind of data replication for ephemeral storage, then a loss of a disk is usually catastrophic to the instance. If the failed disk is where that instance's storage was located, then that data is permanently lost. The instance will need to be terminated and rebuilt.

For block storage, instances may experience problems with the mounted volume. If there are serious issues in the persistent storage cluster, a volume may become unavailable to the instance. If the volume is mounted, any reads and writes may hang, waiting for a response. If the volume is not mounted, it may refuse to mount or be detected as a valid disk. This is seen more often when an instance is being launched or rebooted. If the volume is unavailable for some reason, the instance may fail to launch or need administrator interaction to get the instance to boot the rest of the way.

Most volume issues occur because of issues within the OpenStack environment and not necessarily with the persistent storage cluster. There may be an issue with Cinder or an issue with the communication between Nova and Cinder. Many of these issues may not affect a volume that is already mounted in an instance and currently being used. However, these issues will likely affect the launching or rebooting of instances. This also affects the ability to detach volumes from one instance so that they can be attached to another instance. In most cases, this only affects the ability to access the data and does not result in data loss.

Object storage is accessed in a different manner than for block storage. Objects are pushed into storage or fetched from storage. If there are any issues in the object storage system, it usually manifests as objected being unavailable or operations timing out.

Persistent storage is most often configured with some kind of replication. Replication factors of 2 or 3 are common, but there may be cases where replication is disabled for some reason. It is important to ask the administrators about how replication is configured in order to better understand how failures could affect access to data and the potential for data loss.

Instances have a difficult time dealing with storage devices becoming unavailable. If the application depends on data always being available, it is important that monitoring is configured to monitor storage available and integrity. For ephemeral storage, most failures results in the instance going down as well. However, instances should monitor for when filesystems go into a read-only state. Instances may operate fine with a read-only filesystem, especially if the application only reads data and doesn't write data. Monitoring may not see the issue either, nor will the issue be seen in any of the logs. Since a read-only filesystem is an indication that there is an underlying problem with the compute node, catching it early so the application can adapt around it is a good idea.

Software Failure

Another type of failure scenario is purely software specific. For example, a kernel bug within the operating system of the compute node may cause it to crash or hang. This will result in the instance becoming unavailable. Sometimes, it may be because of a kernel bug in the instance's operating system. The instance itself will crash or hang, requiring a reboot to put it back into operation.

Issues in the OpenStack software suite may also cause problems. Most problems of this nature don't affect an instance, unless it is an issue that will affect the instance's network or ability to access its storage. Common OpenStack software issues include problems with RabbitMQ, Cinder and Ceilometer. These issues may not affect current instances, but they could very likely affect the user's ability to launch new instances, terminate instances, or do any other OpenStack related management. For applications that make use of the elastic nature of the cloud to dynamically grow and shrink instances based on demand, software problems can reduce cloud elasticity significantly.

Another issue that could occur is a lack of resource availability. If an instance is running an application that is leaking memory, that instance will eventually run out of memory and fail. If an application is launching lots of processes and does not properly clean up after itself, the instance can run out of process slots and be unable to launch new processes. If an application fails to close files that it opens and is no longer used and opens a lot of files over time, the application may use up all the available file descriptors. This can cause the application to fail or even possibly the instance. When an instance runs out of resources, it may result in the instance crashing, but it more often results in the instance becoming unavailable. Monitoring may detect multiple alarms and attempts to login may be unsuccessful. Rebooting the instance often fixes the problem. However, if the problem occurs repeatedly, the application needs to be examined for bugs and potential configuration tweaks. It is better to fix the problem with the application than to try solving the problem by launching larger instances with more resources.

External Failures

Instances may experience DNS lookup issues due to some external issue. This could be the result of a network outage between the OpenStack environment and the DNS servers. It could also be an issue with the DNS servers themselves. DNS issues can look like a general network issue from the perspective of the instance. Nearly everything an instance does on the network requires a DNS lookup. When a DNS issue exists, lookups generally do not just fail, rather they timeout. If the instance is configured to do lookups on multiple servers, the timeouts can stack up for each request, compounding problems for applications trying to connect to services on the network.

Instances can reduce the effect that DNS issues have by tuning timeout settings in the /etc/resolv. conf file and by doing some kind of DNS caching inside the instance itself. If caching is used, once a hostname is resolved to an IP address, it will be kept in the cache for a period of time so future DNS lookups for that hostname can be skipped. Many instances are configured without caching enabled. Depending on the operating system installed in the instance, NSCD or dnsmasq may need to be tweaked in order to enable DNS caching.

Another common issue that can occur to instances is its inability to talk to important services on the network. A good example of a common service is an authentication service. Active Directory, LDAP, Kerberos and Radius are all examples of authentication services that could be used. Network issues and issues with the authentication service itself can cause an application to misbehave or fail. Distributed applications may see periodic failures if only a portion of the instances experience authentication issues. For example, users may see a periodic web page failure if their click resulted in an action that talks an instances that is unable to do authentication.

Authentication service issues are difficult to overcome in the instance. The best way to deal with authentication service issues is to detect them when they occur, understand whether or not it is transient or if the issue is trending from bad to worse, and react to the issue. A distributed application could detect authentication issues in a portion of the instances and choose to remove those instances from the pool, working around the problem until authentication service has been restored. At the very least, there should be monitoring that alerts the application owners to the issue so that the root cause can be investigated and the necessary administrators involved.

Instances can also experience issues with time skew. This is a subtle problem that may not be noticed without proper monitoring. Many applications may not even care about time skew, especially for instances that are running portions of an application that does not require state. However, authentication commonly does require the instance's time to be very close to the time the authentication server sees. Some authentication methods are very strict, resulting in failed authentication attempts if the instance's time is more than a minute or two off. Some applications, such as financial applications, require accurate time as well.

Running NTP inside the instances can help keep the instance's clock synchronized to the correct time. However, NTP is not fully reliable, because it depends on the performance of the compute node the instance runs on and it depends on the network performance between the instance and the NTP servers. If the compute node becomes CPU bound, the instance's time may stay out of sync, even with NTP running. By the time NTP adjusts the time for the instance, the adjusted time could be wrong. Network issues can disrupt time updates. The NTP service could also be having an issue. For example, one of the NTP servers could be out of time sync itself and reporting the wrong time. Some of these issues can be solved by configuring the instance to point to several reliable NTP servers. If time synchronization is important to the application's operation, it is essential that monitoring is configured to catch these issues so that appropriate actions can be taken.

HOSTNAME AND IP ADDRESSING

Applications tend to be very complex, and comprised of many functional units, with one unit talking to another. Users also need a way to use the application. This is accomplished by assigning hostnames and IP addresses to all of the difference pieces of an application that need it. An example for a simple application might be a web server that talks to a back-end database. The web server has an IP address that users connect to, and the database has an IP address that the web server talks to.

What happens when the web service is actually a whole bunch of instances? What happens if the database back-end is actually a database cluster running several servers? It would certainly be possible to assign public IPs to all instances so that every single instance is accessible. However, if a user is connecting to the web interface of an application, it would be bad practice to provide all the IPs to the user and force the user to select which one to use.

Single Point of Entry

Normally, an application has a single point of entry for the users. If it is a web application, it is a URL they enter in the web browser. If it is a client/server type application the client is configured to hit a particular server address. What happens when a web application is now a bunch of instances? If the database back-end is several servers running in a cluster, how is the web front-end configured to talk to the database back-end? There are a couple techniques that can be used to deal with application connectivity and the communication between the functional units within the application.

Most applications should have just a single point of entry for connections to come into, which is usually a hostname. When a connection to the application is made using a hostname, the hostname is converted into an IP address through the use of DNS service, which is a service that provides hostname and IP address mappings. The DNS lookup occurs behind the scenes and is transparent to the user or service connecting to the application. The DNS service may return a single IP address or a list of IP addresses for that hostname. An IP address is then chosen and the connection made to the application.

Round Robin DNS

When it comes to assigning more than one IP address to a single hostname, there are a couple techniques that can be employed. The first technique is to use DNS to assign multiple "A records" to the hostname. An A record in DNS is essentially an IP address assignment. When a DNS lookup occurs and there are multiple A records assigned to the name, the DNS server returns all of the IP addresses assigned to that name. However, each time the DNS server is queried, the list is rotated by one so that the first IP address in the list is always different. This is known as "round robin."

For example, the name `myweb` has three A records assigned to it, 1.1.1.1, 2.2.2.2 and 3.3.3.3. The first time DNS is queried, the server responds with `1.1.1.1, 2.2.2.2, 3.3.3.3`. The second time DNS is queried, the server responds with `2.2.2.2, 3.3.3.3, 1.1.1.1`. The third time DNS is queried, the server responds with `3.3.3.3`, `1.1.1.1`, `2.2.2.2`. The fourth time DNS is queried, the server responds with `1.1.1.1`, `2.2.2.2`, `3.3.3.3` again.

The client that is doing the DNS query will get back a list of IP addresses and then has to choose which IP address it will use. Generally, clients always pick the first IP address in the list, which is why the DNS server rotates the list every time the list is returned. However, there is a downside to doing round robin in DNS. If any of the servers in the IP address list is not responding, the client will not know that and will attempt the connection anyways. Clients very rarely have extra logic in their code that tries to connect to the first IP and when that fails, tries the next IP in the list.

It may be difficult for the administrator to react quickly to server unavailability or performance issues. If a server is going to be down for an extended time period, the bad IP address can be pulled out of the list. However, DNS servers are often configured to cache IP address information for a period of time. It is common for DNS entries to be cached for 24 hours or more. If that is the case, removing an IP address from the list could take up to a day or more to be reflected in the DNS queries made by the client.

If a server is going to be down for planned maintenance and the administrator knows that an IP address will need to come out of the list, a common technique is to reduce the cache time to a short period of time, such as 1 minute, well ahead of the scheduled maintenance time. When maintenance is about to begin, the IP can be removed, which clients will see within a minute of the update. Maintenance can occur and the IP address re-added back to the list. If maintenance is successful, the cache time can be adjusted back up to its original setting.

Global Server Load Balancing (GSLB)

Round Robin DNS is a cheap and easy means to allow access to multiple instances that provide an important piece of functionality to an application. It was already mentioned that if one of the instances is down, clients may still try to connect to the instance, being unaware of that issue. However, there are other limitations to Round Robin DNS that can also affect the application. For example, there might be no ability to guide the client in selecting an appropriate IP address out of the list based on performance or possibly how close an instance is to the client.

Global Server Load Balancing (GSLB) is a service that provides a combination of DNS and load balancing functionality. GSLB's are often setup in a similar fashion as Round Robin DNS. A hostname may be assigned to multiple IP addresses. However, instead of the GSLB returning a rotating list of IPs to the client, the GSLB will return the list of IPs in an order that makes the most sense for the client that is doing the DNS query. If an instance is down in the IP list, the GSLB will remove the IP entirely from the list until the instance is back up. IPs are often ordered by geographic location so that the first IP address is physically closest to the client doing the lookup. IPs may also be ordered based on performance or number of connections going to those IPs.

Enterprises may also combine GSLBs with Round Robin DNS and use both techniques. This is useful when an application is hosted at multiple sites. For example, an application hosted in the United States and in Europe could have the GSLB provide only the list of IPs associated with the United States when client from North America queries DNS. Furthermore, the trimmed down list could be rotated in the same fashion as standard Round Robin DNS. Since the GSLB is aware of server uptime and performance, IPs can still be removed when a server is down.

GSLB can be affected by some of the same issues as Round Robin DNS. Since GSLB is essentially providing IPs back to the client via DNS requests, making changes to the list of IP addresses can be affected by cache time. For GSLBs designed for failover when an issue occurs, cache times may be set to small times already. However, clients often cache DNS lookups as well. This means that when an IP address is removed from the list by the GSLB, a client may not notice that until its internal cache has expired for that list.

GSLB provides another level of service beyond what DNS provides by itself. However, GSLB often comes with extra cost, so it may not be feasible to take advantage of it. If GSLB is available, it is the best way to run portions of the application across multiple sites in a reliable way.

Fixed and Floating IP Addresses

OpenStack makes use of two types of IP addresses for its instances. A fixed IP address is automatically assigned by OpenStack when an instance is first launched. The fixed IP address can be either a public or a private address, depending on how the environment is configured. Public addresses allow connections from outside the environment to connect directly to the instances. Private addresses do not allow outside connections, but often do allow connections to other instances within the same environment to be made.

The other type of IP address OpenStack supports is a floating IP address. Floating IP addresses are not automatically assigned to an instance when they are first launched. When OpenStack is configured to use floating IPs, a global floating IP pool is setup with all of the IP addresses permitted to be used as a floating IP. Users will then pull IP addresses out of the global pool and into their tenant pool, marking those IPs as only useable by that specific tenant. Users can then assign IP addresses from their tenant pool to specific instances running in the tenant. Floating IP addresses are most often public IP addresses which allows outside connections to be made to that IP address. OpenStack environments that make use of floating IP addresses will often configure fixed IP addresses to be private addresses and floating IP addresses to be public addresses.

One advantage that floating IP addresses have over fixed IP addresses is that the user can assign and unassign them at any time. The user can move a floating IP address from one instance to another without having to terminate and relaunch an instance. It is also possible to have more than one floating IP address assigned to an instance. This gives the user a lot of flexibility in how a connection comes into the application. If an instance is having problems or crashes, the floating IP address can be moved to a working instance. It is also useful in maintenance. For example, a patch can be applied to all instances. An instance can be patched and then have the floating IP moved to it so that the other instance can be patched without affecting service availability.

Another advantage that floating IPs have is that they can be used as a means to conserve IP address usage in a network. The fixed IP network is often bigger, sized to be larger than the number of instances likely to ever be launched in that environment. The floating IP network may not be as big and may be a finite valuable resource. If that is the case, users could assign floating IPs to only the instances that need outside connectivity and rely only on fixed IPs for instances that only rely on connections inside the environment.

For example, a particular OpenStack setup has a public network assigned to the floating IP addresses and a private internally routed network assigned to the fixed IP addresses. The developer sets up an instance running HAProxy and assigns a floating IP address to it. The developer also sets up a bunch of web instances providing the web front-end for the application. The web instances are configured with fixed IP addresses only and are not accessible from the outside world. The fixed IPs are added to the HAProxy setup and anytime somebody connects to the floating IP's of the HAProxy instance, HAProxy connects to one of the web instances and proxies the traffic between them. If one of the web instances goes down, HAProxy sends traffic to another web instance. If the developer needs to log into any of the web instances, this can be done by first logging into the HAProxy instance and then from there, by logging into the desired web instance.

Neutron Port Reservation

Neutron assigns IP addresses to instances using the concept of port assignments. A port is essentially a virtual switch port that the instance connects to. A port is assigned a MAC address and a fixed IP address. When an instance connects to a port, the instance's network interface inherits the MAC address and IP assignment as well.

By default, when an instance is launched, a port is created with a MAC address and a fixed IP address and then assigned to that instance. When the instance is terminated, the port is destroyed, which frees the fixed IP address up for future use. If floating IPs are not used, there is no way to predict what IP address the instance will get. Nor is it possible to guarantee that if an instance is rebuilt by being terminated and then relaunched that it will get the same IP address it originally had.

Neutron provides a mechanism to allow the user to create a port ahead of time and assign that port to an instance as it is being launched. When the port is created, the user has the option of specifying an IP address or let OpenStack chose the IP address instead. To create a port, use the "neutron port-create" command. When the instance is launched, the port ID of the newly created port can be assigned using `nova boot --nic port-id=PORT_ID`. When the instance come up, it should have a network interface configured using the MAC address and fixed IP address associated with the user-created port.

However, be aware that if the instance is terminated, OpenStack will happily destroy both the instance and any associated port. If the user wants to preserve the IP address associated with the instance, the port must be detached from the instance first before the instance is terminated. This can be done by using `neutron port-update PORT_ID --device_id '' --device_owner ''`. This should work on any port, including a port that was created at the time the instance was launched. After the port is detached, it can be used again when launching another instance.

In older versions of OpenStack, Neutron port reservation wasn't very reliable. Ports could be detached from instances, but they sometimes may not work properly when attached to a newly launched instance, especially if the instance the port was originally attached to is still running. Also, ports could only be attached to instances when they were launched. It may be possible to attach a port to an existing instance by using `neutron port-update`. Consult the OpenStack documentation and test vigorously before using port reservations for production work.

Permanent IP Addresses

Users are accustomed to having a single known IP address associated with their application. A hostname is usually assigned to that IP address, but the IP address rarely changes. Once they have an IP address, firewall ports are opened up specifically for that IP address and that address may potentially be embedded in application code. Of course, if that IP address ever changes, it can be a nightmare to update the application to support that change, as firewalls have to be updated and source code scoured to find all the hardcoded entries.

When users are developing applications for the cloud, it is hard for them to let go of the concept that all their instances should have a permanent IP address assigned. Even if an application is built with multiple instances and regions in mind, users may still have to open firewall ports for all the IP addresses associated with their instances.

If the OpenStack environment supports floating IP addresses, then having a permanent IP may still be possible. If an instance needs to be destroyed and rebuilt, the user can move the floating IP address from the doomed instance to a new one. The firewall rules associated with that IP address continues to work. The same thing can be accomplished by creating and assigning Neutron ports to new instances. However, it is critical to make sure that port is detached from the instance before the instance is terminated, otherwise the port will be destroyed and the IP address put back into the global IP pool.

Another thing users should be cautious of is if an IP address is lost and firewall rules are associated with that address, some other user and application may get that IP address and all the associated firewall rules with it. The other application will have no idea what ports have been opened up in the firewall. This may not be an issue if the security groups are properly set up and restrict inbound traffic. However, it is common for developers to save network security for last or not address it at all and not be aware of the additional exposures that IP address reuse may bring to their application.

SCALING

Once a basic application has been built for the cloud, it needs to evolve so that it can survive failures in the cloud, as well as to grow so that it can continue to meet user demand and performance requirements. Scaling an application vertically may address performance issues, but it rarely improves on its ability to deal with cloud failures. Scaling the application horizontally can address both performance and resiliency to cloud failures.

What does it mean to scale an application horizontally? It means that the application is scaled by adding more instances to it. This is different from vertical scaling where the instances themselves are made bigger. Horizontal scaling doesn't mean making additional copies of the application and running those copies in the cloud. It means taking a single application and spreading it out to run in more instances.

How can an application be spread across multiple instances? The first step is to understand all the different pieces that make up an application and then take each piece and run each of them in their own instance. Then each piece is expanded to run in multiple instances. Some pieces may be easier to run in multiple instances than others. Once an application can scale successfully in a single region, then steps can be taken to scale the application to other regions. An application running in multiple regions can increase performance by having users communicate with instances physically closer to them and increases its resiliency in dealing with potential region-wide outages.

Application Anatomy

Applications are typically very complex, often containing multiple programs working in concert to provide a set of services to the end-user. It is rare to find an application that is a single program that does everything, such as providing a web interface and a database service all in one. Understanding all of the different pieces of an application is important when trying to build and deploy it to the cloud.

Most applications provide some kind of user interface. User interfaces can take many forms, such as a client interface that runs on the user's desktop, a web interface accessed from a browser, a command-line program the user runs from an operating system prompt, or maybe an API that the user uses from within a script or program.

User interfaces provide a mechanism for accessing and manipulating the data the application manages. This data is often stored in a database. Many applications use relational databases that provide better organization and faster access to the data, such as with Oracle and MySQL. Some applications also make use of document store databases, such as with MongoDB. Document store databases provide a means of storing unstructured data and objects. Applications may also make use of multiple databases and database types, further adding to the complexity of the application.

Some applications also make use of an application layer called middleware. Middleware contains software that typically is used to connect application components to other application components. Middleware provides a consistent means of connecting different pieces of the application to each other, making it easier to switch components out for other components in the future.

Applications may have other components too. For example, there may be a network or security component that monitors traffic in some way. There may be a logging component that aggregates the logs of all the other components into a single searchable location. There may be a monitoring component that checks application functionality and performance.

Each component needs to address potential failure scenarios as appropriate. A web-based user interface can deal with failure scenarios by simply scaling out. Since most web-based user interfaces can be stateless with respect to data, instances can be lost with little impact to the application, as long as there are enough instances to handle the incoming load. Databases often deal with failure scenarios by having a number of instances participating in a cluster. As long as the majority of the instances in the cluster remain available, the database is likely to remain up and available.

Each component can also deal with problems independently of each other. For example, if a performance issue is found in the middleware component, that component can be scaled out more to address the performance issue. There isn't a need to scale out the web component or the database component, since the problem was isolated only to the middleware component. Adjusting components independently when needed gives the application tremendous flexibility in dealing with failure scenarios and performance issues.

Multiple Instances

An application that runs in a single instance or in just a few instances is more likely to be affected by simple failure scenarios, such as hardware failure or maintenance. A single compute node failure could rob the application of an important piece of functionality, resulting in users not being able to reach the application or important data being available to them.

The best way to deal with most failure scenarios is to have the application run in as many instances as possible. If one instance in a group goes down, the other instances in that group continue to provide the same functionality so the application remains operational.

Most applications can be broken down into smaller pieces based on functions that can be isolated from other functions. For example, a web-based user interface can often be separated from a database back-end since users do not need direct access to the database and the database doesn't care about how the users see or make use of that data. Breaking an application into smaller functional units is the first step in running an application in multiple instances. The web interface can run in one instance and the database can run in another instance.

Once the application has been broken into smaller functional units and each functional unit separated into multiple instances, the instances can then be scaled out so that each functional unit also runs in multiple instances. For example, the web-based user interface can run in several instances instead of just a single instance.

Running the application across many instances adds a considerable amount of complexity to the application. However, it also provides two key improvements to the application. The first key improvement is that it should make the application more resilient to failures occurring in the cloud. A compute node failure is not likely to take out all the instances of that functional unit. The other key improvement is that it is easier to scale the application horizontally. For example, if user demand increases to the point a particular functional unit is becoming performance-bound or running into resource a limit, the number of instances for that functional unit could be increased to handle the user demand. This not only spreads performance across more instances, but if an instance can only handle a certain number of users, multiple instances can increase the total number of users that can be handled.

Stateless applications are much easier to run in a multiple instance setup. Data kept in an instance is not important enough to protect against loss if there is a failure in the cloud. Furthermore, one instance doesn't depend on data in another instance. If an instance goes away, a user can be routed through another instance seamlessly without having to know what that user was doing in the other instance before that.

Stateful applications are more difficult to run in a multiple instance setup. Data needs to be kept about what is happening and what has already occurred so that what happens next can be determined. For example, you can have a multi-request transaction that is occurring in the application. If all of the requests go through a single instance, the instance has all of the data about the transaction and can handle the transaction end-to-end without difficulty. However, if one request goes through one instance and another request goes through other instances, how does one instance know about the requests that went through the other instances? A stateful application needs to track all the requests of a transaction, no matter how many instances the requests went through.

Multiple Locations

Just as an application needs to run in multiple instances in order to scale and be more resilient to failures in the cloud, the application also needs to be deployed in multiple locations. As discussed previously, there are all kinds of failures that can occur in the cloud, or even outside the cloud, that can affect a cloud application. For example, an outage in the data center can take out an entire location or region. Even if the application runs in many instances, if all of those instances ran in the same location, the application is still unavailable.

It is important to understand the OpenStack environment that the application is going to be deployed to. If there are multiple regions available, find out where the regions are physically located. The application should be deployed to geographically diverse locations, such as on the east coast and on the west coast. If a power or network outage takes out all of the data centers in a particular region, other regions can pick up the load and allow the application to continue operating.

It is also important to understand how regions may differ from each other with respect to speed, redundancy and reliability, and location with respect to the users that may need to use the application. An OpenStack region can be installed in a really nice data center that offers high speed network, lots of bandwidth, power and network redundancy. It can also be installed in a lower tier facility where there may not be as much bandwidth or redundancy, which means that failures could happen more often and have a greater effect on applications deployed there. However, those regions may be closer to the end-user or provide lower latency connections and ultimately provide more plusses than minuses for being in those regions. Knowing how regions differ may result in an application being deployed with fewer instances in one region versus another, or maybe certain functions of an application may be deployed to a higher risk region.

Managing an application that runs in multiple regions is even more complex than just managing an application that runs in multiple instances. Some of the challenges can be reduced if all the requests of a transaction or all the transactions for a user can be kept to the same region. Data access and integrity can also be challenging. If a database is going to run in multiple regions, data needs to be replicated and synced. If the application requires real-time data access, ensuring the data is current in all locations at all times can be difficult, especially if the regions are separated geographically by a large distance.

Load Balancing

Load balancing provides a means to direct traffic flow to those instances that should receive it. In the most basic form, incoming traffic can be split equally to all of the instances, which spreads load evenly and allows for better scaling. In more advanced forms, instances can be monitored so that traffic is split based on availability, performance and level of activity. In particular, if an instance goes down, it can be excluded from receiving additional traffic until that instance is restored back to service.

Load balancers typically provide an easy means to configure how traffic should flow inside an application. A pool is created to monitor a particular service and servers can be added and removed from the pool on the fly. Load balancers monitor the services of each server and determine what traffic should go to it, if any. A pool often has an IP address and port assigned to it. As long as at least one server in the pool is able to receive traffic, the pool's IP address and port is active.

Load balancers monitor the services in a pool by connecting to the service. Monitoring can be as simple as just connecting successfully to the service, or it can be as complex as connecting to the service and expecting a specific banner or string to be returned. Some load balancers provide a means of attaching custom scripts to the checks so that complex checks can be performed, such as authenticating to the service and performing some kind of action. Load balancers can also monitor performance in a way, by looking at how long its checks are taking and basing decisions on that. Successful checks mark the service as available and unsuccessful checks mark the service as unavailable.

Once the load balancer has collected all of the data from the checks performed on the service, it needs to decide how to distribute the incoming traffic. A pool set up to use a round robin algorithm will send traffic to each service, one after the other in sequential rotating fashion. A pool set up to use a least connections algorithm will send traffic to the service that has the fewest active connections. A pool could also be setup to send traffic to the service with the least network latency. More complex algorithms can also be supported, combining simple algorithms, or setting up a priority of services that should get traffic before other services get traffic.

There are many types of load balancers available. Hardware load balancers usually provide the most capabilities, reliability and ability to handle large amounts of traffic. However, they are also more expensive than any other type of load balancer. Also, hardware load balancers managed by another team may add additional complexity to its use. Nonetheless, if hardware load balancers are available, it is recommended to take advantage of them.

Software load balancers are cheaper and can be more flexible than hardware load balancers. You can build and incorporate software load balancers into the application, tightly coupling how load balancing is done with the needs of the application. There are many types of software load balancers. One of the more popular choices is HAProxy. There are a number of load balancers available using Apache and Java as well.

OpenStack also provides a Load-Balancing-as-a-Service (LBaaS), which is implemented using Neutron. It supports many of the same features that regular load balancers support, such as service monitoring, management of the services in the pool, managing connection limits, and providing session persistence. Check with the OpenStack cloud administrators to see if LBaaS is available and how it can be used.

One of the things that need to be considered when setting up load balancing for an application is what kind of traffic will be going through it. Not all network protocols may be supported by load balancers. If session tracking is used, either the application needs to share session information across all of the needed servers, or the load balancer needs to be configured to send a single session's traffic to the same back-end server until that session is terminated.

Another thing to be considered is that load balancing will increase logging quite a bit on the servers in the pool. Generally, load balancers like to check services every few seconds to make sure they are up. In an enterprise environment, there may be two or more load balancers configured identically, all of them checking every few seconds on those same services. Unless the application is configured to not log those connections, logs can grow quite a bit.

Ultimately, load balancing provides a valuable way to improve an application. It provides a means to monitor the services and remove servers from a pool that are no longer working. It also provides a means to add and remove servers on the fly, which is an important part of application scalability.

Performance

When an application is architected so that its various pieces can scale to multiple instances and those different types of instances can scale independently of each other, the complexity of the application increases dramatically. When problems occur within the application, it becomes more difficult to identify where the problem is actually occurring. Sometimes, problems manifest as broken functionality within the application. However, more often than not, problems manifest as performance issues.

What kind of performance issues could an application experience? Performance issues can take many forms. For example, a backup system has to backup all the data of an application every night and has to be completed before the next business day. However, over time, backups are taking longer and eventually risk not finishing in time. Another example maybe an application that accepts file uploads and it has to virus check the application before confirming to the user it was successful. It may be that virus checking is taking longer and longer and uploads are failing because they are timing out or the user doesn't wait around long enough for it to complete.

Application performance is often characterized as the amount of time to perform specific actions. For example, a web user clicking on a link within a web page will expect the click to immediately respond with a new page and expect to see the new page completely loaded within a short period of time. Perceived slowness can sometimes be attributed to the accumulation of all the different things that has to happen behind the scenes. If a single-user click results in twenty different actions occurring, each action may be quick, but the total time to process all twenty actions may be too long.

It is incredibly important to monitor every aspect of an application. Data can be collected on how long database transactions take. Data can be collected on how long data is transferred over the network or written to disk. Data can be collected on the number of successful or failed events. Data can be collected on number of connections and logins. All of this data should be collected over time so that it can be analyzed for potential issues and understood in context with other events, such as holidays, special events or abnormally high usage.

When performance issues are discovered, a number of things can be done. Some performance issues may be related to higher activity and can be solved by simply adding more instances to the pool to handle it. Other performance issues may be related to a change in the usage pattern. For example, users may be searching on something in a different way, and the SQL query created to do that search is somehow searching inefficiently in the database. Fine tuning the search capability or creating a new index in the database or fine tuning database settings may be the more appropriate way to fix the performance issue than simply adding more instances to the database service.

Operating system performance should also be heavily monitored. For Linux servers, it is a good idea to run SAR and collect data on CPU, memory and disk performance. A good metric to monitor is the CPU steal time, which can be seen in the SAR data as %steal. If this value is consistently non-zero, it usually means CPU cycles are being stolen from that instance and given to another. Looking at that metric in combination with the %idle metric and looking at these values across all the instances collectively can provide clues as to whether the hypervisor is overloaded or that maybe the instance is undersized.

OpenStack provides some metrics data for application developers to take advantage of. Ceilometer collects information about CPU and RAM usage, disk activity, network bandwidth and other data. It is possible that Monasca is being used as well, which provides many of the same metrics as Ceilometer. Be sure to talk with the OpenStack cloud administrators to see if metrics are being collected in the cloud and how they can be used by the application.

Data Storage

In OpenStack there are a number of different ways that data can be stored. By default, when an instance is launched, it uses ephemeral storage. Ephemeral storage is usually storage associated with the compute nodes where the instance runs. If the instance is terminated, all the ephemeral storage associated with that instance is also deleted. Ephemeral storage is the least protected data within OpenStack. The storage is likely not backed up or replicated. A lost disk or compute node could lead to data loss.

Block storage is provided by Cinder in OpenStack and presents that storage as volumes that can be attached to the instances. Volumes show up as block devices inside the instances and can be mounted as disks or filesystems. Volumes can be attached, unattached and moved to different instances. When an instance is terminated, the volumes are detached from the instance and is not deleted. The volume can then be attached to a new instance if need be. Block storage is implemented in Cinder through the use of drivers, many of which are vendor specific. Very often, block storage is set up to be performant and to replicate data to prevent issues resulting in data loss.

Object storage is provided by OpenStack through the Swift API. Data is stored in a completely different way than with block storage. The application creates containers and then uploads files into those containers. Access to the files requires them to be downloaded from the container and into the instance. Containers and their associated files have no concept of instances. If an instance that uses a container is terminated, nothing happens to the containers or its files, remaining accessible by other instances in the cloud. In fact, one of the advantages Swift has over Cinder is that containers can be accessed by many instances, but a block storage volume can only be attached and accessed by only one instance at a time. Object storage is also often set up to be performant and to replicate data to protect against data loss.

When building an application that needs to store data permanently, selecting the appropriate data storage back-end is extremely important. How important is the data? Is it okay for the data to be lost if an instance dies? Can the data be replaced or rebuilt if a new instance is created? How long is the data needed? Does the data need to be always immediately available? How much data needs to be stored? These questions can play a big role in deciding what is used to store data and how it is stored. Be sure to talk to the storage administrators to better understand the available options. In particular, discuss with them about their data replication settings, how much storage they have and what your application's long term needs are so they can plan accordingly.

If data is stored in an environment that replicates data, the application should take care not to do its own data replication. If the storage cluster replicates data three times and the application is also replicating data three times, this really means that the data is being stored a total of nine times in the cluster! This can affect application performance due to unnecessary replication, as well as consume way more disk space than is really needed.

Applications can take advantage of multiple storage options at the same time. Since ephemeral storage is often faster than using block or object storage, an instance can keep its more often used data on ephemeral storage and the less used data on block storage. Data that is rarely used could be put into object storage for long term storage. Be sure to consider all options when building an application that requires storing data.

High Availability

To build an application for high availability in mind means that the application has to be available as much as possible and that it needs to run properly and performant at all times. A highly available application often runs everywhere and is able to adapt to the changes in the environment where it runs. Building an application is hard enough, but building a highly available application is even harder.

What are some of the techniques involved in running a highly available application? One of the most important techniques is to ensure the application and all of its pieces can run in many instances, and that those instances can also run in multiple environments. The more places the application runs in, the more resilient to hardware or even data center failures. Multiple instances also allows the application to scale appropriately as needed.

Another technique is to put services behind load balancers so that traffic can be appropriately distributed. Furthermore, if any instances become unavailable, the load balancers will automatically remove those services from the pool and redistribute traffic to the remaining services. Using GSLB can also further increase high availability by redirecting traffic to different data centers based on were connections are coming from. If a data center goes offline, GLSBs can automatically redirect all traffic to another data center until the issue is resolved.

It is also wise to understand application usage and how that ties in with the bigger picture. External events can cause significant increases in traffic usage. Holidays can result in increases for holiday shopping, especially on days like Black Friday and Cyber Monday. Sporting events, like the Super Bowl, can increase web site activity for viewing on-demand data. Universities can see increased activity associated with the beginning of the school year or changes in quarters and semesters. Major news events could drive up stock activity. All of these need to be considered when building an application for high availability. Ideally, if an event can be anticipated ahead of time, the application can be scaled upwards accordingly ahead of that event to deal with expected demand and then scaled back down after that event has passed.

How can the application scale to meet demand? One way is for somebody to actively monitor the services and manually add instances as needed until the application can handle that need. This can be an expensive way to address the problem and introduces a human element and risk to the overall process. Another and better way is to monitor the applications for problems and performance and auto-scale the application in a pragmatic way. OpenStack provides many APIs for managing instances and services in the cloud. The application can detect when it needs to grow a particular service and use the API to do that. When demand subsides, the application can reduce the number of instances running in an automatic way.

Another important thing to consider is building in extra capacity in the application ahead of time. Instead of expecting each instance to be 100 percent busy and only deploy the number of instances needed to handle all of the load, build each instance to be 60 percent busy and run more instances. One advantage to this strategy is that brief spikes in capacity can occur that might not trigger auto-scaling. With extra headroom built into the instances themselves, spikes can be handled without causing any issues with performance in the application. The key is to over-provision and under-utilize.

High availability does present other challenges though. Taking a look at a case where a particular service runs in multiple instances with one instance acting as a master and the other instances acting in a passive role. Very often, the instances are talking to each other all the time, ensuring the master is alive and well. What happens if something breaks the communication between the master and passive instances? The master may not be aware of this issue and continues to operate normally. The passive instance sees the master go away and immediately puts itself into master mode. What if the other passive instance does the same exact thing? There could be three master servers all at the same time. This is commonly known as split-brain syndrome and can be a hard problem to avoid in certain failure scenarios. This problem can be even more pronounced between regions when network communication is disrupted.

Now, we're going to see how we can implement what we've discussed in this chapter to improve our sample application.

IMPROVING OUR APPLICATION

Starting with the simple application concept introduced in the previous chapter, we want to build on that and show how it can be improved upon. Conceptually, the process isn't that difficult. However, not all of it is easy either. For example, an application that requires persistent sessions needs to work in a multi-instance environment. In any case, if the application can be broken into its basic components, each component can be improved upon independently and in a way that makes the most sense for that component.

Simple Application

Let's take the application that was started in the previous chapter. The application has three components to it: a web-based front-end that users will access, an API layer that the front-end talks to, and a database back-end. The application may look something like Figure 5-1.

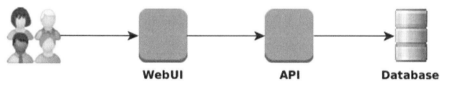

WebUI   **API**   **Database**

FIGURE 5-1

Initially, the application may have been kept simple in order to provide a proof of concept so the application is viable in the cloud and to seek approval for continuing its development. Each component may exist as a single instance. For the above example, the application would exist in three instances, one for each of the different components.

Complex Application

The above example could be considered overly simplistic. More complex applications may use an API layer to abstract access to multiple types of back-ends. The API provides a consistent means to access different types of data, making it easier to extend functionality or even to allow back-ends to be swapped out without having to recode any of the front-ends. The API could also take input from more than just a web front-end. Users could access the API using command line tools or a client program. This application may look like Figure 5-2.

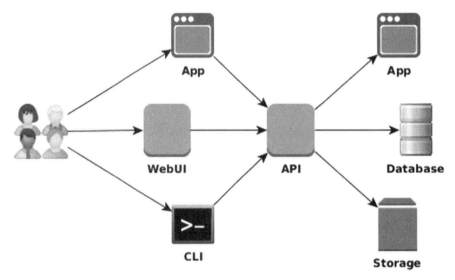

FIGURE 5-2

When looking at the components to build this application, it turns out that it really isn't that complex. The API layer is still just a single instance. The web front-end and the database are also each their own instance. The client program and command line tools don't need their own instances. They are just abstract methods for the user to access the API directly. The API can also access file storage directly and communicate to other applications in the environment. The end result is that this application is still only three instances, even with more "stuff" going on with it.

Improving the Web UI Component

In order to improve on the web front-end, the application needs to be scaled out to multiple instances. The number of users expected to use the application can be used as a guideline to determine the number of instances that likely will be needed to run the web front-end. Also, users need a consistent means of accessing the web service without having to worry about which instance they are connecting to. This is accomplished by putting the web instances behind a load balancer (see Figure 5-3).

FIGURE 5-3

One challenge that may need to be addressed when putting a web service behind a load balancer is when the web service does session management in order to track user activity during the lifetime of the session. A session starts with the user logging into the web service and gets assigned a Session ID. The user's Session ID may be tracked by embedding it in the URLs or a hidden form, or maybe even through the use of web browser cookies. The web service maintains information about the session while the user is logged in. The session ends when the user logs out or there is no activity from the user after some time.

The difficulty with session management is often in its implementation. What happens if a user logs in using one instance, but the next click on a web page sends the user to a different instance. How is session information shared between instances? If session information is stored locally within an instance, other instances may not even have that user's information.

Most load balancers have a way of dealing with this issue, implementing a feature called session affinity, persistent sessions, or sticky sessions. One method used in the feature assigns the source IP of the user to a specific instance and all traffic coming from that source IP will always go to that instance. Another method uses a tracking cookie the load balancer creates and assigns all traffic containing that cookie to a specific instance. One drawback by using session persistence in a load balancer is that pinning traffic to specific instances significantly reduces the load balancer's ability to balance traffic in meaningful ways. Over time, some instances may be significantly busier than other instances simply because of how users are using the application. If an instance becomes overloaded, adding more instances to the Web UI layer may not help because those users are permanently pinned to the overloaded instance.

The best way to deal with session management using multiple instances is to abstract session management to a shared database that all instances can access. If session information is not kept locally within an instance, it no longer matters which instance the user hits or even if the users hits multiple instances in the same session. This also avoids the problem that load balancers have with persistent sessions, since user traffic is not pinned to specific instances. The drawback, however, is that the database used to store session information needs to also be implemented in a highly available manner. This prevents a single database instance from breaking the web interface completely.

Improving the API Component

In order to improve on the API layer, it also needs to be scaled out to multiple instances. The number of instances can be chosen based on how performant the API instance is in dealing with incoming connections, communicating with its various back-ends, and passing that data back to the requesting sources. Since the API layer is often implemented using similar technologies employed by the web front-end, the method for running the API using multiple instances is similar to that used by the web front-end. This is accomplished by putting the API layer behind a load balancer (see Figure 5-4).

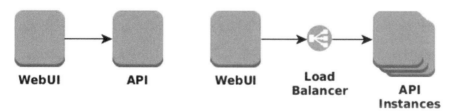

WebUI   **API**   **WebUI**   **Load Balancer**   **API Instances**

FIGURE 5-4

One advantage that the API layer often has over the web front-end is that it doesn't have to keep track of user sessions. This makes it easier to run multiple instances behind the load balancer, since it doesn't matter which API instance is being hit at any particular time.

However, APIs may implement their own form of session management through the use of an authentication token. The user receives the authentication token when they authenticate successfully with the API. The user can then use that token in each follow-up call to the API without having to authenticate each request. After a period of time, the token may expire and force the user to re-authenticate, which either renews the token or gives the user a new token.

The API layer often manages authentication tokens using a back-end database. This means that if a database is being used, the database needs to be highly available in order to prevent a single database instance from disrupting API functionality. If the API is only making use of the database for token management, the API could continue to function without tokens, forcing users to authenticate each API request.

Improving the Database Component

For the database layer, scaling the database out to more instances is not as simples as just running multiple copies of the database instance. For the web and API layers, the instances really do not need to know anything about the other instances in that layer. There could be a single, several or many web and API instances and the application would run the same way.

So, how can the database layer be improved? The database layer is scaled out, but it is scaled on a much smaller level. Where the web and API layers may have hundreds of instances, the database layer may only have a few instances. The database instances often replicate data so that each instance is identical to the other. It is how the data is replicated that makes the database layer more complex. There are a couple different ways that the database layer can be put together to provide redundancy and increased performance.

One of the more popular methods for scaling the database layer is to run a Galera Cluster for MySQL. A Galera Cluster allows multiple MySQL instances to communicate to each other and replicate data. It runs in multimaster mode, which means that read/write communication can occur with any instance in the cluster. When a transaction is committed, the data is replicated to all instances and returns successfully only when that data was written to all of the databases successfully (see Figure 5-5).

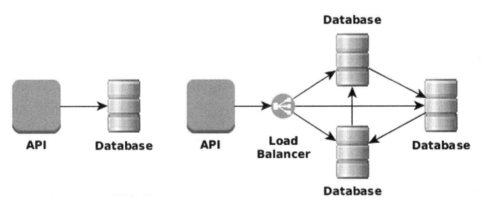

FIGURE 5-5

Another method for scaling the database layer is to run a MySQL Cluster. Generally, MySQL Clusters are setup in two different sets of nodes, the SQL nodes and the data nodes. The API layer talks to the SQL nodes, which determines where the data is stored and then makes the necessary queries to the appropriate data nodes. The data can be split into smaller chunks, called partitions, and stored on a subset of the data nodes. Replication occurs within pairs of data nodes within the cluster. The more data nodes there are, the more partitions there are, spreading the data across the entire cluster (see Figure 5-6).

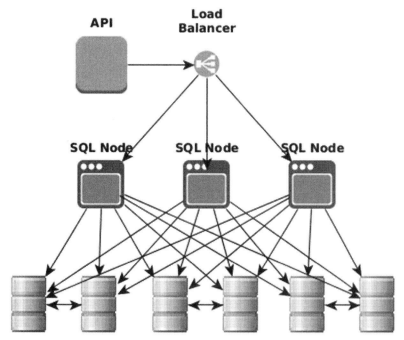

FIGURE 5-6

One advantage of running a MySQL Cluster is that it can scale to more instances. The more instances that are added, the more the data can be spread across that cluster. However, MySQL Cluster is more sensitive to latencies and requires more CPU and network resources to run efficiently. The application may also need to be reworked to take advantage of the partitioning of data, otherwise, a single query could hit every data node and result in a potentially worse performance.

For Galera MySQL Cluster, it requires very little change from the application point of view. There is no data partitioning, so every instance has a complete copy of the data. This can also be a drawback, however, since the more instances there are in the cluster, the more data that has to be replicated to every other instance. This is generally why Galera Clusters are small, usually at least three instances, but not much larger. Another consideration when running a Galera Cluster is that there always has to be at least 50 percent of the instances running in the cluster at any point in time. If the cluster drops below 50 percent, the entire cluster stops and the database goes offline. It can sometimes be difficult to bring the cluster back online without making changes to the cluster configuration files. This is why a cluster needs to have at least three instances in it. If one instance is lost, there is still majority in the cluster to keep it operational.

Yet another method combines the concept of a cluster above with multiple read-only databases on the back-end. This is typically called a write-master/read-slave setup. If the application needs to write data, the writes always go to the write-master database. If the application needs to read data, then the reads are farmed out to any number of available read-slaves. The write-master could be set up as a Galera Cluster or MySQL Cluster, which the read-slaves could be setup as standalone MySQL servers in a non-clustered setup. It is not uncommon to see the read-slaves use caching software, such as with Memcached, to further speed up reads. A load balancer could be used to evenly distribute reads across all the read-slaves. When a read-slave is initially launched, it can pull down whatever data from the write-master it needs to have and once all the data is loaded and verified, it can add itself to the read-slave collective and take on traffic. This model is more complicated, but it does provide more flexibility in regards to scaling (see Figure 5-7).

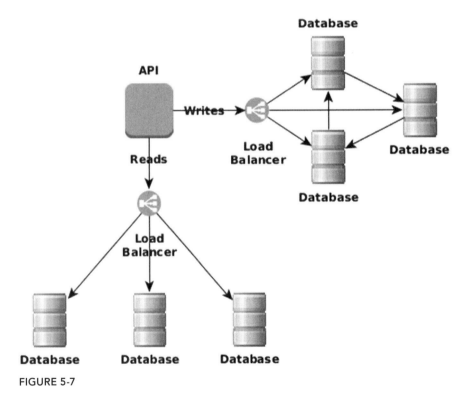

FIGURE 5-7

The above examples use MySQL as the example database. Other databases can also be put into the OpenStack cloud as well, and with similar types of configurations. For example, MongoDB and PostgreSQL support native clustering and replication. Some databases even have native support for the master-write/read-slave model. In general, you should research what types of capabilities the chosen database solution has and take advantage of whatever high availability options it provides.

Finally, it would be remiss to point out another potential database layer improvement, which is to take advantage of Database-as-a-Service (DBaaS). In OpenStack, this is Trove, which was discussed previously in Chapter 2. If there is a DBaaS solution available for the OpenStack cloud, take a look at what features it provides and how it can be leveraged in the application. Offloading the database piece to another service simplifies the application tremendously and provides the additional high availability and data protection needed without having to reinvent the wheel.

Putting It All Together

Now that each of the layers has been examined, it is time to put them all together. Users come into the application via a single location, the load balancer, which is then routed to one of several Web UI instances. The Web UI layer talks to the API instances through a load balancer as well, each API request distributed amongst all the API instances. The API layer talks to the database through a load balancer to a back-end cluster (see Figure 5-8). The cluster is set up as multimaster, allowing any database instance to be hit by the API instances.

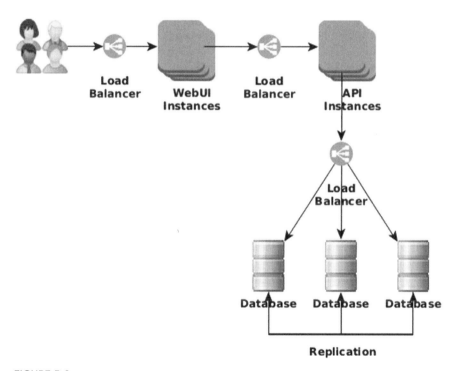

FIGURE 5-8

Multi-Region Instances

Many of the improvements listed above are typically applied at a region level, where all the instances are in the same region. It is possible that parts of the application exist in multiple regions. For example, the Web UI and API layers may exist in one region, but the database layer is in another region. However, ideally, all of the layers need to run in multiple regions.

The main trick to running any layer in multiple regions is load balancing. Each layer in each region still has its own load balancer, but then there is a global load balancer that routes traffic to each of the regional load balancers. If a GSLB is able to be used, it is a perfect use case for spreading an application across multiple regions, since traffic can be redirected to the nearest geographically located region to the user. Figure 5-9 shows an example of how the Web UI or API layer can be organized to work in a multi-region OpenStack cloud.

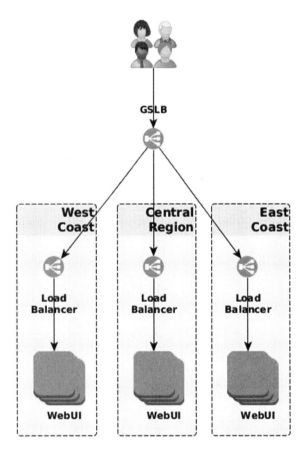

FIGURE 5-9

For the database layer, it similarly uses the GSLB to redirect traffic to the nearest geographically located database. Instead of abstracting each of the regions to their own set of load balancers and database clusters, however, it can be simplified by treating the GSLB as the main load balancer and all the regional databases as database instances within the same cluster. Another simplification that comes from this setup is that only two database instances are needed for each region, since even if a single instance goes down, there are plenty of instances across all the regions to ensure more than 50 percent of the cluster is up. Figure 5-10 shows an example of a multi-region database setup.

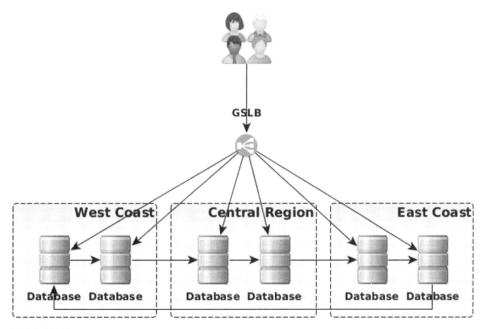

FIGURE 5-10

SUMMARY

We have now pulled together our example app created for the OpenStack cloud. It is a good idea, however, to assume that the cloud is a hostile environment, presenting risk to the application's uptime and the integrity of its data. Knowing what kinds of things can happen to the application and what kinds of failures that can occur in the cloud opens the door to improving the application to be able to survive when things do happen.

One of the basic improvements that applications undergo in the cloud is to enable the application to scale when it needs to. The application needs to scale horizontally within a region and it needs to scale out to multiple regions. This gives more resilience to the application so that pieces of it shutting down don't take out the whole application. Using load balancers as part of the scaling also gives the application a type of self-healing capability, allowing pieces of the application that are no longer accessible or functioning properly to be removed from the pools so that users don't inadvertently try to use them.

When looking at the individual components of an application, some pieces of the application need to be improved in different ways than other pieces. For example, web components can be scaled out without much effort. However, database components typically can't be scaled out as much, since scaling can make it more difficult to manage the data behind it and affect performance. Databases can be scaled out, but they are scaled out differently than how the web component is scaled out. Databases are best managed as a cluster of instances and this chapter presented several ways that databases can be run in the cloud.

The suggestions presented in this chapter are just the tip of the iceberg. There are a number of different ways an application can be improved, and developers are encouraged to reach out to the OpenStack community and research techniques that other developers are using when building applications for the cloud. The next, and final, chapter takes the cloud application to the next level, since simply building an application for the cloud is not enough to just run it there. Deploying the application to the cloud in an automated, dynamic way also brings challenges to the developer.

Deploying the Application

WHAT'S IN THIS CHAPTER?

➤ An overview of the different virtualization technologies and how deployment varies between them

➤ A look at the orchestration tools available in OpenStack

➤ A discussion on the role of configuration management

➤ The minimum role of monitoring in a cloud deployment

➤ A dive into application scaling and elasticity

➤ An example of how to put all of this together and deploy a modern app in an OpenStack-driven system

➤ Considerations for updating and patching

Devops is a term you have probably heard of recently. It's a description of someone (or a team of people) who tackles the issues of both developing an application and configuring/maintaining the environment for that application.

For years, the role of a server administrator has been quite different from that of an application programmer. Each role takes a pretty specific skillset, and a lot can be said about devops being a difficult compromise. The term however, could not be better suited to what it's like to deploy applications in an OpenStack-driven environment.

When we talk about deploying an application to the cloud, it has a slightly different definition than what it has traditionally meant. Traditional deployments are often focused on deploying changes to an application, or on the initial deployment of a piece of software. OpenStack and other cloud-based technologies, however, make it possible to programmatically deploy software along with all of the servers, storage, and networking necessary to run that application.

As you will see, this has a number of advantages and can be accomplished in a number of different ways. This chapter will take a look at these technologies, how to choose between them, and how to use them to quickly deploy an elastic application—something nearly impossible to do in a hardware-based world. We will then conclude with a short discussion about how this new definition of deployment affects the traditional process of patching and updating software.

BARE METAL, VIRTUAL MACHINES, AND CONTAINERS

Before you can determine *how* you're going to deploy, you first have to determine *what* you're going to deploy. Looking at the demo application developed in Chapters 4 and 5, the first thing that needs to be deployed is a number of servers. What wasn't discussed much in those chapters, though, was what type of virtualization those servers would use.

In the same way OpenStack allows those who implement it to choose their own hypervisor, storage devices, and networking equipment, it also allows developers to determine for themselves what type of virtualization they want to use for any given project/application. Instances, or servers, can be launched as a completely physical computer, as a virtual machine (VM) running in a hypervisor, or as a container—an isolated processing space that can exist on top of a virtual machine or on top of actual hardware.

The choice you make between these three technologies will be the biggest determinant of how you deploy your application. You will find staunch defenders of each, but the choice is often a subtle exercise in compromise and personal preference. Thus, it's important to understand their differences before moving forward.

Bare Metal

Bare metal provisioning is exactly what it sounds like: the creation of a server on physical hardware. As of the Juno release of OpenStack, bare metal provisioning has been moved from the Nova driver to its own service called Ironic. Hardware is registered through the Ironic API, but once properly configured, servers are still deployed in the same manner as virtual machines though the Nova API or Horizon (see Figure 6-1).

Bare metal servers are primarily used when you need the absolute highest performance and stability possible. While the overhead of virtual machines and containers has dropped over the years, there is no such thing as software that doesn't consume memory and processor time. Disk IO, and CPU priority are all guaranteed in a bare metal scenario. Bare metal servers are also a good option if GPUs or other hardware devices that can't be easily virtualized are part of your application.

Additionally, even if performance isn't of the highest concern, there are times for regulatory purposes, when you might find it necessary to deploy bare metal servers anyway. Hardware isolation provides the absolute maximum amount of server security in any OpenStack-driven environment.

That being said, if performance and isolation are the upside, then efficiency and flexibility are its main downsides. Bare metal servers cannot be subdivided beyond their hardwired components. This either tends to leave a lot of underutilized hardware out there, or results in developers piggybacking multiple applications onto each physical server.

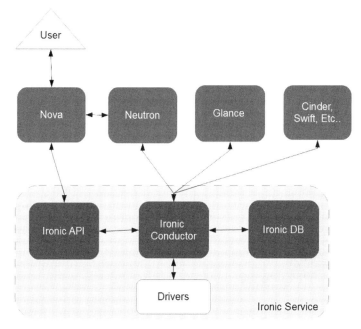

FIGURE 6-1

To upgrade an application running on bare metal to bigger hardware often means taking it down while physical changes are made, or having a large variety of hardware on hand. This comes with its own set of headaches, and removes many of the benefits provided by a system like OpenStack. The ability to start small, grow instantly, and offer numerous isolated environments, are all great reasons to look at other virtualization options.

Virtual Machines

From the perspective of deploying a server in OpenStack, virtual machines are still the industry standard at the moment. Multiple virtual machines run on top of a single hypervisor that itself runs on top of a single operating system residing on a single piece of physical hardware (see Figure 6-2).

The biggest advantages to virtual machines were already touched on earlier in this chapter. Virtual machines allow you to split one large physical server into many smaller isolated servers. These can each have a unique configuration and running application. This avoids piggybacking and helps prevent one application from taking down another that runs on the same server.

Upgrading or downgrading a virtual server is also a simple matter of asking OpenStack for a different flavor. This is not only handy for testing and tuning application performance, but can drastically reduce the amount of hardware required for any given environment. After all, there is no need to plan for the worst when you can instantly deploy a new server with more resources.

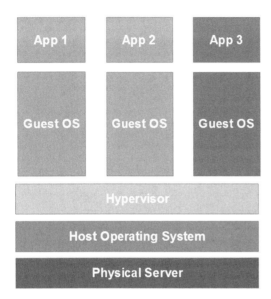

FIGURE 6-2

Of course there are trade-offs when it comes to this kind of virtualization. While OpenStack can be configured to allow for over-subscription of resources, generally speaking, once either all of the memory, CPU, or drive-space has been allotted from a given piece of hardware, the remaining assets cannot be assigned to another instance and essentially go to waste. It is also possible for the scheduler to fail to find a single piece of hardware that meets all of the requested criteria. For example, even if a cluster has hundreds of free gigabytes (GBs) of RAM total, if no single box has more than 15GB free and a 16GB server is requested, then the creation will fail. This is a good reason to always deploy the smallest computing unit possible.

Some efficiency is also lost due to the hypervisor. While there have been great improvements in this technology over the years, routing calls to and from the host OS and devices isn't free. The overhead here is difficult to calculate and can vary based on the OS, device, and the software involved, but can easily reach as high as 15 percent. For smaller environments, this doesn't amount to much, but for larger installations, this can become a deal breaker. Enter containers.

Containers

Containers are the new belle of the ball. While they are based on old technology (various forms of containers have been around for years), the introduction a few years ago of the Docker toolset to easily create new containers, spurred the big players (Google, Amazon, and Microsoft) to begin adopting the technology.

There are several types of container including LXC, BSD Jails, and OpenVZ. LXC has gained the most traction and can be packaged in several formats—Docker and Rocket being the most common. There are some growing differences between these container types, formats and packaging technologies, but generally speaking they all do the same thing. They each offer software that creates virtual environments mimicking a full virtual machine. The trick is that each container is missing the main OS kernel. Calls to the kernel are instead sent from each container to a single daemon, which runs on a single instance of the host OS on each physical server. This means the overhead of having multiple kernels in a VM scenario is gone (See Figure 6-3).

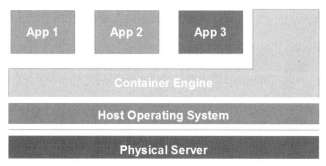

FIGURE 6-3

There is no denying that containers have many advantages over virtual machines or bare metal deployments. Containers allow for the code of an application to be deployed simultaneously with its server configuration as the container image can contain both. They deploy much faster than a full OS image, as they are only a fraction of the size (as small as a few MBs), and they can provide an exact copy of an application (and its configuration) for development or testing (this can be a positive or a negative in truth).

Depending on whom you ask, and the specifics of your application, containers can also be much faster than their hypervisor-driven counterparts. The native host OS kernel and scheduler decide which processes get CPU time instead of having to go through one scheduler per VM and then another scheduler where the host OS determines which VM process gets CPU time. Greater density can also be achieved through the use of containers. Smaller images and fewer kernels in memory mean smaller computing units and great cost savings at scale.

Generally speaking, the renewed excitement surrounding containers is well deserved, but it's important to acknowledge that they are not a silver bullet for OpenStack Deployments.

Containers on a machine (or pod) must share the exact same kernel/operating system. This has repercussions if an application needs to modify the kernel, or if there is a desire to host various operating systems (or versions) on a single piece of hardware.

There are also some security concerns when deploying containers if any of them are to be given to an untrusted source. Exploits where a user escapes their container and breaks into another have been recently demonstrated and reinforce the fact that containers are not a one-size-fits-all solution, at least not yet.

The biggest hurdle with containers, however, is that they aren't yet available as first order objects within OpenStack. For now, containers have to be deployed and configured on top of virtual machines that are themselves managed by OpenStack. The diagram for this looks a little different (See Figure 6-4).

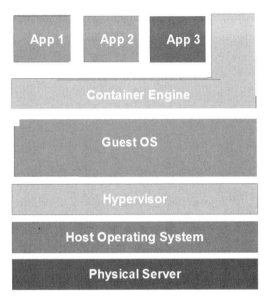

FIGURE 6-4

This can provide the same level of isolation/security as VMs if each customer is given their own VM to run their containers on, but OpenStack is essentially unaware of containers in this scenario. Resizing and provisioning containers has to be done outside of Nova. Additional configuration outside of Neutron is needed to create private networks and handle inbound access. Containers can't be managed or visualized within Horizon, and the performance penalty of a hypervisor in addition to the container daemon actually makes them less performant than virtual machines alone.

There are some impressive third-party options like Cloudshift and Cloudify that can provide container management in this configuration. However, this still happens outside of OpenStack, and it remains to be seen what place these tools will have once containers on bare metal becomes available.

Containers on Bare Metal

When people speak about containers on bare metal in an OpenStack-driven environment, they are generally not *just* referring to the concept of running containers directly on the host OS.

This could theoretically be achieved by provisioning a bare metal server, loading on a standard Linux distribution (or a more dedicated one for containers such as CoreOS or RancherOS), and running Docker or another container system on top of that. This idea has some advantages over bare metal alone, like being able to subdivide hardware. Unfortunately, it still lacks the orchestration and management capabilities provided by OpenStack.

More often, when someone speaks about containers on bare metal, they are referring to several new projects that attempt to provide both the efficiency of eliminating the hypervisor as well as enabling OpenStack to manage these containers as first order objects.

One of these projects, Magnum, was discussed earlier in Chapter 3. It has been available since Kilo-2 and makes orchestration engines like Google's Kubernetes and Docker's Swarm available for container management. The paradigm is slightly different and involves things like "pods" and "bays," but generally speaking, it provides virtual machine–style management for containers that run directly on host operating systems.

In theory, containers on bare metal provide the best of all worlds. You get the efficiency/density of containers, the native management of VMs, and (according to some early benchmarks) nearly bare metal performance.

Unfortunately, as with a lot of revolutionary technology, Magnum isn't always available, and supported orchestration engines like swarm, Mesos, and Kubernetes could still use some time to mature and stabilize. There are also some third-party options outside of Mangum/OpenStack like Cloudify that provide interesting solutions and support, but, you will likely find yourself choosing between bare metal, virtual machines, and classically managed containers for quite some time.

Choosing the Right Technology for the Problem

From a deployment perspective, virtual machines are usually the easiest way to go. Unlike bare metal, they are efficient, and can be scaled up with a command. Unlike traditional containers they can be managed natively through OpenStack's Horizon and the various APIs. Unlike bare metal containers, the technology is mature, and Nova/Compute (as opposed to Magnum) is definitely available.

In our demo application, there are no specific requirements for custom hardware or GPU utilization in either the web or rest tiers. Neither of these seem to require hardware level performance, nor do they need hardware level isolation, so bare metal isn't really necessary. If local drives are used, its sometimes popular to use bare metal in MySQL servers (for performance reasons), but generally speaking this isn't an issue as long as they are provisioned with enough memory to keep them from accessing the disk too frequently. We also won't be deploying enough servers in any of these tiers that the smaller overhead of Containers will really come into play. This leaves us little reason to choose anything other than to deploy standard virtual machines in all cases here.

If this were a real production project, you would want to consider a few other things before making the decision: What kind of expertise is available on your team? What options are available in your OpenStack environment? Are you going to distribute this application internally or elsewhere? The answer to these questions should impact your decision. Most of the time, a single choice will make things easier, but a mixed environment is also a reasonable response. Certain systems (Hadoop, MySql, etc.) may benefit from the maximized performance and stability of bare metal provisioning, while you may want to deploy preconfigured containers or empty virtual machines for other components.

Whatever you choose, consider how this will affect your deployment. For example, some tools like Heat are only available to first order objects like virtual machines and not containers (for now). Alternatively choosing bare metal may require you to piggyback some of your application on to a single server. Regardless, the remaining subjects in this chapter: orchestration, configuration, and scaling are built on the foundation of this initial choice, so choose wisely.

ORCHESTRATION AND CONFIGURATION MANAGEMENT

Now that a virtualization technology has been chosen for each of our server types, they actually need to be provisioned and configured. The network for the application also needs to be setup and appropriate security groups and restrictions put in place. This was all done manually in the examples in Chapters 4 and 5, but in practice it's important to look at deploying a cloud application as more than just using OpenStack as a self-service portal for server provisioning (IAAS) and/or a series of available services (PAAS). Embracing the ability to script the construction of your environment has huge advantages. Meanwhile, treating your application as if it lives within a classic environment (deploying and configuring it the same way) can result in absolute disaster.

In a classically provisioned environment, you might be given access to a powerful server, spend several hours/days/weeks manually configuring it, and then deploy your application to that server. This works moderately well. Modern servers are built with hard drive arrays, multiple power supplies, and have fault tolerant ram. In the event of a failure, the hope is that the redundant components can take over and downtime can be avoided.

As was discussed earlier in Chapter 5, resilience in a cloud-based application doesn't rely on redundant hardware. Instead, commodity hardware is often used, and multiple servers and isolated application tiers creates resiliency. Expecting any given server to lock up, stop taking requests, or just disappear is all part of the plan. Even if more robust hardware were used, when it just takes the push of a button to permanently delete all of your carefully configured servers, it is important to be able to recreate them quickly.

This is why scripting the orchestration and configuration of your environment is a vital part of deploying any cloud-based application. Doing this not only provides the previously described benefits, but it also ensures consistency between servers, self-documents, and is a perfect opportunity to work on your devops skills. It is also the basis for adding elasticity to our demo application, as you will see shortly.

Orchestration Tools: Heat, Murano, Cloudify, and More

Much like we needed to look at all of the virtualization options before determining *what* was going to be deployed, it's important to look at all of the orchestration options before making a decision on *how* these things are going to be deployed. With respect to this, there are a number of options that are commonly employed that are all referred to as orchestration techniques or tools.

The first of these is just to create your own script from scratch. There is nothing to stop you from doing this in the language of your choice. The compute, networking, and platform APIs provide all of the basics you need. As long as a 1:1 ratio is kept between applications and Keystone projects, Horizon will even provide you with a pretty clear visualization/inspection of your environment. This is a perfectly viable option, and though it requires a lot of initial effort up front, it is a common orchestration solution. It is especially useful when dealing with components or services that exist outside of OpenStack.

As far as integrated solutions go, Heat (being the main orchestration component of OpenStack) is the obvious choice. Its template files allow you to describe your environment in a well-documented manner. Using Heat eliminates some of the grunt work of manual scripting, such as having to provide detailed output and error handling. Heat also supports several different configuration management options, making the next step in the deployment process easier still.

Murano is another option for somewhat programmatic orchestration. As discussed earlier, it provides both an application catalog, as well as a way to zip up applications for third-party consumption. Packaging an application for Murano along with all the wizards and scripted orchestration is generally overkill though, unless you are planning on distributing to users in other OpenStack environments. Ultimately, Murano is more about distribution than it is about orchestration, and so it is not generally a recommended deployment mechanism for custom applications.

Of course, no concept in OpenStack would be complete without a healthy dose of third-party applications that provide alternate solutions. Cloud Foundry and Cloudify both offer orchestration. If these are available within your OpenStack installation they are definitely worth a look. Their success is due in part to their friendlier UI and their ability to simplify the orchestration process. However, because they communicate to OpenStack via the same native APIs you have access to, there is little they can accomplish that you can't accomplish yourself with a little manual scripting work or through Heat.

Lastly, there are new companies, such as Rancher Labs and projects like Kubernetes and Mesos, that are starting to provide container-focused orchestration solutions that live on top of, or work with, OpenStack. These are the bleeding edge of virtualization technology and as such are likely to see huge changes before mainstream adoption. They are, however, worth mentioning in case you are looking for a container-focused solution, need to span multiple clouds, and/or have experience using Rocket, Docker or similar technology.

Since we have chosen to use virtual machines over containers for our demo application, and the application isn't meant for wide distribution, that leaves two good choices for orchestration: manual scripting and Heat. If the demo was a more complex application or if there were components that simply could not be managed within Heat, then raw scripting would be the go-to solution. It is also possible to use Heat as a component of a larger script, as it is essentially an API as well. As is though, Heat is reasonably well documented and provides a single simplified system for communicating to all of the different OpenStack components the demo application is going to use. This makes it the best choice for now and the remainder of this book will focus on the use of Heat templates for deployment.

Configuration Management and Cloud Init

If orchestration is anything that occurs *above* the server level, configuration management can generally be considered to be anything that needs to be modified at the server level or below in order to get your application up and running. Adding specific software, updating configuration files, or even pulling down an application from Git occurs under the umbrella of configuration management. In the case of the demo application, this could mean Apache for the web tier or Node.js/Python for the Rest layer and MySQL for the database(s) along with all of their respective configuration files.

Before we get into tools like Puppet and Chef, which really are the standard for configuration management these days, there is another option called Cloud-Init that is well worth your time to explore. Technically speaking, it is just a Linux package that handles early initialization of a cloud instance. From a developer (or devops) perspective, it is also one of the simplest ways to run scripts after a server has been provisioned.

What you choose to do in these scripts and/or what language you want to employ is up to you. Cloud-Init simply runs what you tell it to either by including the script under `user_data` as part of your API call to Nova, or though Heat as follows:

```
heat_template_version: 2014-10-16
description: Simple template to deploy a single compute instance
parameters:
 image_id:
  type: string
  label: Image ID
  description: Image to be used for compute instance

resources:
 web_server:
  type: OS::Nova::Server
  properties:
   image: { get_param: image_id }
       flavor: m1.small
   user_data_format: RAW
   user_data:
    #!/bin/bash
    echo "You just ran this command!"
```

In this example the server would first be provisioned, and then the command in user_data would be executed and "You just ran this command," would be output to the command line. This can actually be viewed though the spice-console once it is available in Horizon as part of the boot sequence.

It should be pretty easy to see how you could expand on this concept to configure a server to meet your needs. Instead of manually installing XYZ after provisioning it, you could simply write a script to install XYZ and include it as part of your Heat template. A slightly more useful example might look like the following:

```
heat_template_version: 2014-10-16
description: Simple template to deploy a single compute instance
parameters:
 image_id:
  type: string
  label: Image ID
  description: Image to be used for compute instance

resources:
 web_server:
  type: OS::Nova::Server
  properties:
   image: { get_param: image_id }
       flavor: m1.small
   user_data_format: RAW
   user_data:
    #!/bin/bash
    yum install -qy git
    yum install -qy npm

    git clone https:/github.com/folder/package.git /var/usr/share/app
    node /usr/share/app/server.js

    echo "You just installed and started a node app!"
```

Creating a stack with this template would provision a single small server with the specified image. It would then be configured with Git and NPM (Node.js), so you can download a project from GitHub and start it. For our demo application, different installation and configuration scripts would be inserted for each of the server types.

Depending on your OpenStack configuration and your base image, Cloud-Init's Cloud config Yaml format may also be available. It provides some excellent functionality without having to write a lot of code. Converting our earlier example would result in something like:

```
heat_template_version: 2014-10-16
description: Simple template to deploy a single compute instance
parameters:
 image_id:
  type: string
  label: Image ID
  description: Image to be used for compute instance

resources:
 web_server:
  type: OS::Nova::Server
  properties:
   image: { get_param: image_id }
      flavor: m1.small
   user_data_format: RAW
   user_data:
    runcmd:
     - yum install -qy git
     - yum install -qy npm
     - git clone https:/github.com/folder/package.git /var/usr/share/app
     - node /usr/share/app/server.js
     - echo "You just installed and started a node app!"
```

This is a pretty simple example, but it is a fairly complex and powerful system. For further reading on Cloud-Init and some great examples of how to configure a server with the Cloud config format take a look at `http://cloudinit.readthedocs.org/en/latest/topics/examples.html`.

Puppet, Chef, Salt, and Ansible

While Cloud-Init is a general system for running scripts for whatever purpose you like, there are numerous tools dedicated solely to configuration management. Puppet, Chef, Salt, and Ansible aren't the only options in this realm, but they are definitely the biggest players, and they have some important similarities and differences to consider if they are to be used as part of an OpenStack-backed deployment.

First off, all of these applications share the idea of plug and play modules (called *recipes* in Chef, and *playbooks* in Ansible). These prebuilt blocks are the biggest thing that differentiates them from configuring a server with Bash or other scripting tools like Cloud-Init. Modules are available from public repositories that anyone can submit to or retrieve from, similar to PIP in Python or NPM in Node.js. Additionally, they have all attempted to come up with a simple language/structure for describing a server's configuration, handle installation errors, and provide different configurations for servers in different roles. The formats are familiar—JSON, YAML, etc., but the actual syntax and methodology are proprietary and not portable across solutions.

The language they were built upon, their need to have installed clients (Ansible, for example, doesn't need one), and the breadth and depth of their module libraries, are really what differentiates these tools from each other. As with most technologies, you will find enthusiastic supporters and dissenters of each, but for most purposes they are equivalent. In fact, their similarity, and the ability to develop a generic syntax for their use, is a big reason why there is growing support for all of these tools within OpenStack.

Let's look at what a simple Puppet Manifest might look like to configure a server to run Apache and PHP:

```
# install apache
package { 'apache2':
 ensure => installed
}

# start apache and ensure its running
service { 'apache2':,
 require => Package['apache2'],
 ensure => running
}

# install php
package { 'php5':
 require => Package['apache2'],
 ensure => installed
}

#create an info.php file to show that this all worked
file { '/var/www/html/info.php':
 ensure => file,
 content => '<?php phpinfo(); ?>',
 mode => 0444,
 require => Package['php5']
}
```

With the Puppet client correctly installed and the preceding file saved as manifest.pp, you could then execute this template as follows:

```
$ sudo puppet apply ./manifest.pp
```

Puppet deals with any error handling, determines the order things have to happen in based upon the require statements, and handles all of the differences in OS types. For example, using these tools, you don't have to write one script for CentOS that installs software via Yum, and another version that supports apt-get installation on Debian or Ubuntu.

As was mentioned before, Heat actually provides hooks for all of these tools in the form of a SofwareConfig resource. If your configuration supports Chef, then a Heat template to set up Wordpress might look like this:

```
resources:
 wordpress_config:
  type: OS::Heat::SoftwareConfig::Chef
  properties:
```

```
cookbook: http://www.mycompanycom/hot/chef/wordpress.zip
role: wordpress
# input parameters that the chef role(s) need
inputs:
 wp_admin_user:
  type: string
  mapping: wordpress/admin_user
 wp_admin_pw:
  type: string
  mapping: wordpress/admin_password
 db_endpoint_url:
  type: string
  mapping: wordpress/db_url
 # various other input parameters …
# Have chef output the final wordpress url
outputs:
 wp_url:
  type: string
  mapping: wordpress/url
```

From the OpenStack documentation at `https://wiki.openstack.org/wiki/Heat/Blueprints/ hot-software-config-spec`:

> *The resource type OS::Heat::SoftwareConfig::Chef indicates that this is a Chef-specific Software Config definition. The cookbook property points to the used Chef cookbook, and the role property points to the role to be set up via this Software Config. The inputs section contains the definition of input parameters that have to be passed to Chef for configuring the role. Input parameters are defined in terms of name and type. In addition, a mapping specifies to which role attribute the respective input parameters needs to be assigned (i.e. Chef-specific metadata).*

If this seems confusing, don't worry. This example is simply meant to show the developers behind OpenStack are aware of these tools, and that if you are familiar with them, there are a number of ways to tightly integrate them into your deployment. Again, exactly how you choose to configure your servers and your application is entirely up to you. Your company and/or your operations team may have a lot to say on the subject, or the choice might be yours alone. What's important is to have a general understating of the options available and form a game plan.

With that in mind, let's to go over two other important pieces of functionality that all of these configuration management solutions provide. First off, they offer centralized management of servers. Once the client is installed, and the server has been registered into the master, you can use a web interface to do things like search for a server, see what software is installed, or even push/schedule a patch for it (see Figure 6-5).

This configuration isn't required though, and these tools can all be used in masterless mode where this central authority is entirely absent. There is a lot of crossover between what these centralized systems and what OpenStack/Horizon can offer, so it's not unusual to use them in this masterless manner.

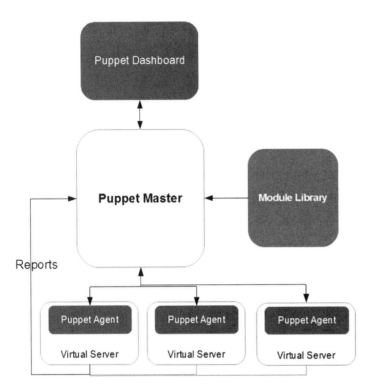

FIGURE 6-5

The other piece of functionality they all offer is the ability to execute arbitrary commands on remote servers. This is an aspect of the same mechanism that allows the master servers to patch remote computers. Ansible in particular can be an indispensible tool when used for this purpose.

Unlike Puppet, Chef, and Salt (to some extent), Ansible doesn't require the installation of a specialized client to support remote command execution. It uses SSH and private/public keys to achieve a similar result. It is also easy to configure Ansible with a local file to push these commands to many servers at once (as opposed to sequentially). This makes remote execution quick and easy from any computer with Ansible installed. A configuration file for Ansible looks like this:

```
[devservers]
dev.cloud.mycompany.com

[prodservers]
prod01.cloud.mycompany.com
prod02.cloud.mycompany.com
prod03.cloud.mycompany.com

[otherservers]
server1.cloud.mycompany.com
server2.cloud.mycompany.com
```

This file defines three groups of servers (devservers, prodservers, and otherservers). Commands can be run on an individual box, a group, or all groups at once. You can also determine how many servers to run the command on simultaneously. So if, for example, you want to update Git on all of your production servers at once you could run:

```
$ ansible prodservers -a "yum update -yq git" -f 3 -u myusername ↵
    --sudo --ask-sudo-pass -i /myuser/ansible_hosts
```

Since Yum often requires sudo access, the `ask-sudo-pass` value has been invoked, and `-f 3` indicates that you want to run it on three servers at once. If there were 6 servers defined in the `prodservers` group, then it would run this in two separate batches. This is often useful to avoid things like cache slamming or to avoid rebooting all of your servers at once, making your application temporarily unavailable.

Ansible is highly recommended as an easy way to execute remote commands, but this does not make it a shoe-in for the configuration solution for our demo application. In fact, there is one drastically different option to consider.

Where Do Snapshots Fit In? Or Should They?

With all of these configuration options it's valid to ask where images fit in to a deployment. Rather than script the configuration of a server or several servers with different roles, it is definitely possible to take a snapshot of a server once it's configured and simply deploy it in this configured state. While there are a few caveats to that and/or building a custom image, this will usually work. Images can be uploaded through Horizon or through the Glance API, and a number of pre-configured images are available from companies like Bitnami to make this even easier. Generally speaking though, this isn't a great solution.

Images are bulky and cumbersome. If you want to modify a single value in a single file, you can end up having to re-create an entire image all over again. This is actually one of the main problems that Docker is attempting to solve with the DockerFile container system. Testing changes, debugging, and even storing all these images can be a time and space consuming process. Configuration scripts on the other hand, act like tiny zip files that expand on a server to create fully configured boxes. They are easy to edit, store, and version. Depending on the software involved, it's even possible to use the same script to configure windows and Linux boxes.

There are at least a few situations, though, where creating custom images can be an extremely effective solution. If you are not using containers, your configuration scripts take a long time to run, and you are deploying them frequently, then using images or snapshots can be a much faster option. This is often the case with large windows builds. .NET components and enterprise class windows software can take hours to completely install and get running. Images can also be useful way to distribute software. Ensuring software such as Puppet, or Git is already installed can prevent any number of teams from having to install and configure these items themselves. In this scenario, a combination of pre-configured images and post provisioning configuration scripts are used effectively.

Because the needs of our demo application are relatively simple, and the tools are native to OpenStack, the rest of this chapter will focus on using Cloud-Init and `user_data` within Heat to handle server configuration. This will keep things light, and won't require a deep knowledge of any of the configuration management tools. When it comes to your own application though, we encourage you to experiment and choose what works best for you, your team, and your application.

MONITORING AND METERING

It might seem odd at this point to begin a discussion on monitoring. We have yet to even look at a complete deployment solution. However, monitoring is a pre-requisite of elasticity and required to some extent to make scaling useful. After all, without knowing the load on a system, it's hard to know if you need to increase the server or stack size. This holds true even if such changes are done manually or programmatically.

You may also find if PAAS or external components aren't used, that your deployment actually includes its own monitoring system. This may seem a little Inception-like, but it's not very complicated in practice. Monitoring servers can be deployed and configured in a second project, stack, or even serially before the application servers within the same project. It is also likely, if you work within a larger company, that some sort of centralized monitoring is available for you to use.

OpenStack does have a couple of built-in monitoring options that can be useful for deployments. Monasca is a PAAS component that offers monitoring as a service. It consists of a number of sub-components: an agent that runs on each server, a CLI to speak to the Monasca REST API, a storage system for metrics, an alert system, and an analysis engine that enables the alerts and a number of other features.

The result of collaboration between HP and Rackspace, Monasca, can be a capable, but stunningly complex monitoring solution. For a full explanation and some interesting reading, visit `https://wiki.openstack.org/wiki/Monasca`.

The other first-party system that offers some level of monitoring is Ceilometer. Ceilometer is discussed in Chapter 3. It was primarily built as a telemetry service to measure utilization and to store that data for later analysis. Like Monasca, Ceilometer can measure things like load, and trigger alerts when certain thresholds are met. Unlike Monasca, it can also report detailed information on things like how much processor time was used by a given virtual machine or project. The most straightforward use of this is to enable usage based billing or metering. You may find it useful for things like comparing the efficiency of server configurations or determining which applications are over provisioned. Further documentation on Ceilometer can be found at `https://wiki.openstack.org/wiki/Ceilometer`.

If you are looking for an off the shelf solution that isn't integrated with OpensStack (or, as is often the case, these services are not available), then both Nagios and Sensu are worth a look. These solutions both function by adding a client to each server that you want to monitor and deploying a centralized monitoring server that collates this data and displays it within a web based GUI. Similar to Puppet and Chef, there are community submitted checks that can be run on the client servers. These commonly watch things like CPU use and available memory and send results or alerts to handlers on the central hub. There are also a number of community-built handlers available to send things like SMS or email messages, or log results to a database for later analysis.

Nagios is currently free for up to seven monitored servers, while Sensu (being the new kid on the block) is free for the non-enterprise version. Both of these systems are completely scriptable and can thus provide any level of monitoring necessary, as well as any functionality required to trigger elastic changes within the application.

Generally speaking, it's hard to recommend any of these as great solutions. Monasca should be a slam dunk, but it's rather enigmatic and Ceilometer doesn't provide a lot of flexibility when compared to systems like Sensu and Nagios. Meanwhile, the external solutions both offer good usability, but aren't natively integrated with OpenStack. Adding these to our demo application for example, would mean deploying and configuring the central servers and clients as well.

Ceilometer alerts, though, are fairly well documented and can be configured and used within Heat templates to enable some level of elasticity. For that reason alone it's the best choice for the demo application. In a real world scenario you would want to see performance graphs, and be able to log and alert your team members to specific app related metrics (such as the number of connections or session counts). As a free solution, Sensu is probably a great place to start if you need to push beyond what will be demonstrated here.

ELASTICITY

As mentioned in Chapter 5, elasticity is the idea that applications can programmatically shrink and grow to match load. In a non-cloud scenario, the size and/or number of servers deployed are generally determined by the maximum capacity you want to accommodate. In an elastic cloud app, the size and/or number of servers should ideally be the minimum required to accommodate the current load, and grow to the maximum that can be afforded as load increases. This is slightly different than scalability, which is simply an applications capacity to grow.

The primary motivation behind elasticity is that using the absolute minimum computing units needed at any point in time can lead to great savings at scale. Even if you aren't paying by the server at a hosted solution, being able to scale up only the applications that need it at any time can lead to drastically smaller server rooms.

There are other benefits as well, though, beyond cost savings. Elasticity and resiliency are very intertwined. Instead of dealing with downtime on an application that is getting too much traffic, elastic applications automatically grow to meet demand and stay alive. They can also be forced scale up in order handle hardware and network failures even in times of low/moderate traffic. Using concepts like anti-affinity (basically using servers in different racks) an elastic app is also easier to keep running while applying patches, or when servicing hardware. Additional sets of servers can be made available to use while sets of them are taken down for maintenance.

Of course, not everything needs to be elastic.

Making Sure You Need Scaling/Elasticity

Something you won't hear much of is that not all applications need to scale. Not scaling isn't interesting. Not scaling isn't cool. Not scaling won't win you any awards. However, if you can avoid scaling, then you can focus your efforts elsewhere and greatly simplify your deployment. Some examples of applications or environments that may not need to scale:

➤ **Intranet websites:** These see limited traffic and downtime doesn't affect customers.

➤ **Post processing systems:** Systems that analyze data or crunch numbers can benefit from scaling up and going faster, but if it's not mission critical and you can wait for the result, then faster results aren't always worth the effort.

➤   **Single/Fixed Server Applications:** Generally speaking, there is still plenty of software only runs well on big, fast, stable hardware and can provide speed benefits when extra memory/processor is present. If the requirements of your application won't allow for distributed computing across multiple servers, and it can soak up as many resources as you can give it, then go as big as you can on a single instance and move on.

Even if your application, or a given tier of your application, does not fit into one of these categories and you want it to scale, this does not mean it needs to be elastic. Elasticity is great for cost savings and can allow your application to grow rapidly without your intervention, but that is not always desirable or necessary. Elasticity adds yet another layer to an already complicated list of technologies and takes time and energy to implement and perfect. Some situations that may not be appropriate for elasticity include:

➤   **Anything that receives manic traffic patterns:** Spinning up new servers is fast, but even when using containers there is some latency. The same can be said about spinning them down. Load balancing changes and configuration updates can also take time to complete. If you have to deal with quick, massive fluctuations in traffic, it's best to simply plan for maximum capacity and let it run 24/7.

➤   **When working with no budget:** If you're lucky enough to have no budget then it's one less thing on the todo list. Simply scale up beyond anything reasonable and add more compute if things ever get close to max capacity and run with a big margin of error at all times.

➤   **When working with fixed budgets:** It's unnecessary to grow an application if there is no budget to pay for additional servers. It's also unfortunately common to loose budget if less servers are used for a given period of time. If you absolutely need fixed costs for fixed periods of time, then a scalable but non-elastic application is a reasonable way to go. You can just scale things manually each quarter or when the budget changes.

➤   **When a there is a non-elastic bottleneck:** There is no point in quickly scaling your app up and down to handle traffic if an external factor limits the utility in this. If your application has a non-elastic throttle then consider scaling manually to match this.

In the end, if it's possible to scale your application, it's worth considering doing so, and doing so programmatically in an elastic fashion as part of your deployment. If you want to see all the benefits from a cloud deployment, then this is all but mandatory. Both your custom applications, as well as many off the shelf systems can gain speed, resilience, and cost savings if you do.

Looking once again at our demo application, it's easy to see that the user facing web tier as well as the Rest tier could both benefit from elastic scaling. The database layer though isn't quite as scalable and would not immediately benefit in performance from additional servers. It's also not a trivial process to add a server to an existing Galrea cluster as the replication can take a long time to catch up. So this is good example of an application that is entirely scalable, but only benefits from elasticity on several of the components.

Scripting Vertical Versus Horizontal Scaling

Before you can add elasticity to an application, it must first be scalable. Before you can scale, you must first determine the type of scaling you want to use. The simplest form of this is just to increase the size of the servers involved, adding more CPU, Ram, or Disk (depending on the application). This is called vertical scaling, and can be applied to almost any application right out of the box.

By letting you define the Flavor (size) of any given instance when you provision the server, OpensStack makes vertical scaling rather easy. It's worth noting that not all OpenStack setups will let you increase the size of an existing server, and it is almost always necessary to create a new instance if the desired size is smaller. As long as your deployment is scripted though, it shouldn't be hard to create and configure a new server.

Imagine you were using the following heat template:

```
heat_template_version: 2014-10-16
description: Simple template to deploy a single compute instance
parameters:
 flavor_size:
  type: string
  label: Flavor Size
  description: The size fo the flavor to be used

resources:
 web_server:
  type: OS::Nova::Server
  properties:
   image: CentOS6_64
   flavor: { get_param: flavor_size }
```

Saving the file to `test.yaml` and running the following command would create the smallest server possible:

```
$ heat stack-create test_stack -f test.yaml -P "flavor_size=m1.tiny"
```

To scale this vertically to a larger instance you could simply call:

```
$ heat stack-update test_stack -f test.yaml -P "flavor_size=m1.large"
```

Heat would then handle the call into Nova to increase the size of this instance and your application would have that much more horsepower to run with. Horizontal scaling is a little more complicated.

Horizontal scaling involves adding extra servers to an application, usually behind a load balancer that handles the initial request and routes it to an individual instance. This can add the complexity of provisioning and configuring the load balancer as part of your deployment, but scaling an application horizontally usually provides much greater capacity. It's not uncommon to run hundreds of servers dedicated to a specific purpose in a horizontally scaled application. The limit of a vertically scaled application meanwhile is the maximum size of a single instance/flavor. Vertically scaled applications also miss out on the resiliency and maintainability added by the extra servers involved.

In Chapter 5 we determined that both the web tier, as well as the API tier, should both use horizontal scaling. It will provide much greater capacity, and the application will benefit from the added resiliency that the separate servers provide. That being said, it's worth noting that most of the techniques that follow can also be applied to scaling in a limited vertical fashion. After all, throwing hardware at the problem is sometimes the fastest solution.

Load Balancing Revisited

Chapter 5 discusses load balancing in depth. Hardware solutions such as A10, software solutions such as HAProxy, and load balancing as a service (LBAAS) though Neutron are all options. Your choice here as well will greatly affect your deployment solution.

Most of these solutions have APIs that can be tapped into by either the orchestration or configuration management solutions. As when using third party solutions for monitoring, it may also be necessary to include the provisioning and configuration of your load balancer as part of your deployment. HAProxy solutions often look like this, as the proxy server can simply be another VM within an OpenStack project.

If LBAAS is available and functioning correctly in your OpenStack installation, it is a great option. It is easily configurable via Heat, and/or can be tapped directly via the Neutron API. This is still relatively immature technology though, and for many people, hardware or software solutions are the only option.

The deployment of our demo application will focus on LBAAS and Neutron. As time goes on, this solution is only going to get better and be more widely available. In the meantime, if for any reason you need to create your own solution, HAProxy is a decent choice. It does expose a single point of failure, as it generally exists on single machine, but it is available to everyone for free, and it makes the automatic addition or removal of servers relatively easy.

A nearly infinite amount of information on how to install and configure HAProxy is available at `http://www.haproxy.org/`. Assuming that it is already deployed and configured, the following Node.js script demonstrates a basic auto-update concept that could eliminate the need to update your load balancer as part of your deployment:

```
#!/usr/bin/env node

var HAProxy = require("haproxy");
var OSWrap = require("openstack-wrapper");
var FS = require("fs");

var user = 'my_username';
var pass = 'my_password';
var pid = 'my_project_id';
var kurl = 'keystone_url';
var proxy_cfg ='/etc/haproxy/haproxy.cfg';

var haproxy = new HAProxy('optional/socket/path.sock', {});

OSWrap.getSimpleProject(user, pass, pid, kurl, function(error, project){
  if(error){console.error(error);return;}
  project.nova.listServers(error, server_array){
    if(error){console.error(error);return;}
    FS.writeFileSync('/etc/haproxy/haproxy.cfg', '
listen app *:80 \n
    mode http \n
    balance roundrobin \n
    option httpclose \n', 'utf8');
  var ip = '';
  for(var i = 0; i < server_array.length; i++)
```

```
{
 //assuming only one network and a fixed ip
 for each(network in server_array[i].addresses)
 {ip = network[0].addr; break;}
 FS.appendFileSync(proxy_cfg, 'server '+i+' '+ip+':80\n', 'utf8');
 }

 haproxy.reload(function(error){
  if(error){console.log(error);return;}
 });
 });
});
```

Installing this as a cron job on the proxy server would cause it to contact your OpenStack installation every X minutes, retrieve a list of servers, write them to the configuration file, and hot reload the proxy with the new configuration file.

With the decision on load balancing out of the way, and either handled via LBAAS/Neutron or automatically via HAProxy, we can move forward and look more closely at some options for programmatically scaling our application.

Scaling with Heat and ResourceGroups

As opposed to defining every server as an individual entry, Heat templates allow you to specify a ResourceGroup and the number of duplicates that you would like of that resource. Reworking our Heat template from earlier, we get:

```
heat_template_version: 2014-10-16
description: Template to mulitple servers of the same kind
parameters:
 server_count:
  type: number
  label: Server Count
  description: The number of servers do deploy

resources:
 tiny_cluster:
  type: OS::Heat::ResourceGroup
  properties:
   count: { get_param: server_count }
   resource_def:
    type: OS::Nova::Server
    properties:
     image: CentOS6_64
     flavor: m1.tiny
     user_data_format: RAW
     user_data:
      runcmd:
       - yum install -qy git
       - yum install -qy npm
       - git clone https:/github.com/folder/package.git /var/usr/share/app
       - node /usr/share/app/server.js
       - echo "You just installed and started a node app!"
```

Saving the file to `group.yaml` and running the following command would create the smallest server possible:

```
$ heat stack-create group_stack -f group.yaml -P "server_count=2"
```

To increase the number of servers in this stack to four you could call:

```
$ heat stack-update group_stack -f group.yaml -P "server_count=4"
```

Using this technique, different types of ResourceGroups can be defined for each tier of the demo application and each ResourceGroup can be scaled independently. This concept provides a deployment solution that covers everything except load balancing, monitoring, and elasticity. These things have been left out because it is quite possible one or more of them in your application will have to be handled outside the realm of OpenStack. The good news is that if you find yourself in this situation, Heat and ResourceGroups can still be used in this fashion as part of a broader deployment script. The other technologies discussed in this chapter, such as an external A10, can then be included in that script to fill out the deployment solution.

If you are lucky though, and LBAAS through Neutron is available along with Ceilometer alerts, you have a complete deployment solution for elastic scaling that fits neatly within a Heat template.

Putting It All Together with Heat, Ceilometer, and AutoScalingGroups

Before we go into the final example and demonstrate a complete solution for deploying an elastic application, let's review the choices that have been made in this chapter regarding how the demo application will be deployed.

➤ **Virtualization**—Virtual Machines for all three tiers

➤ **Orchestration**—Heat

➤ **Configuration Management**—Cloud-Init/user_data

➤ **Monitoring**—Ceilometer

➤ **Scaling**—Horizontal for all three tiers

➤ **Elasticity**—Viable for the web and API tiers

➤ **Load Balancing**—Neutron/LBAAS

With that in mind let's look at another example. This one will consist of two different files. The first, will describe a single server as a resource. For the second, a parent file will use this resource as part of an auto-scaling group:

```
heat_template_version: 2014-10-16
description: Simple Web Server + Load Balancer Member
parameters:
 network:
  type: string
  description: the network all of the servers will use
 pool_id:
```

```
  type: string
  description: the load balancer pool
 parent_stack_id:
  type: string
  description: the ID of the calling stack
resources:
 server:
  type: OS::Nova::Server
  properties:
   flavor: m1.tiny
   image: cirros-0.3.4-x86_64-uec
   metadata: {"metering.stack": {get_param: parent_stack_id}}
   networks: [{network: {get_param: network} }]
   user_data_format: RAW
   user_data: |
    #!/bin/sh

    # A tiny HTTP server that responds with the IP address of the server.

    IP='ip -f inet addr | grep inet | grep -v 127.0.0.1 | awk '{print $2}' ↵
    | cut -d / -f 1'
    LENGTH='echo x$IP | wc -c'
    cat > /tmp/http-response <<EOF
    HTTP/1.0 200 OK
    Content-Type: text/plain
    Content-Length: $LENGTH

    $IP
    EOF

    unix2dos /tmp/http-response
    nohup nc -p 80 -s $IP -n -lk -e cat /tmp/http-response &

    # now, let's add some load to trigger CPU alarms
    # find a number of seconds to burn based upon IP address
    # this way different ones will burn CPU at different times
    # 60, 180, 300, 420 seconds at a time
    # then sleep 120s
    SECONDS='echo $IP | awk -F . '{print 60 + $4 % 4 * 120}''
    cat > /tmp/load.sh <<EOF
    #!/bin/sh

    while [ 1 ]
    do
    if [ "0" -eq \'echo | awk '{print systime() % $SECONDS}'\' ]; then
     sleep 120
    fi
    done
    EOF
    chmod 777 /tmp/load.sh
    # cirros does something weird to /bin/sh so we need something else to run us
    # later - and there is no "at"
    nohup watch -t /tmp/load.sh &
 member:
  type: OS::Neutron::PoolMember
```

```
      properties:
        pool_id: {get_param: pool_id}
        address: {get_attr: [server, first_address]}
        protocol_port: 80
```

Let's call this file `web-server.yaml`. Looking at it briefly, it takes parameters that describe which network and load balancing pool to use as well as a parameter to define the parent stack this server will exist on. All of these parameters will actually be supplied by the parent template, which we will look at momentarily. First though, it's important to go over what's being configured in `user_data`. As part of the Cloud-Init, this server will be configured to run a little HTTP service that just returns the private IP of the instance. So, when you call from the load balancer VIP, you can see which instance handled the request. Each instance also runs a background process that alternately burns CPU for anywhere from 60-480 seconds, depending on its IP address, and then sleeps for 120 seconds. This simulates load and triggers the elastic scaling up and down.

As for the main/parent heat template, that would look something like this:

```
heat_template_version: 2014-10-16
description: AutoScaling Web Application
parameters:
  network:
    type: string
    description: the network all of the servers will use
  subnet_id:
    type: string
    description: the load balancer subnet
  external_network_id:
    type: string
    description: the UUID of the external Neutron network
resources:
  web_server_group:
    type: OS::Heat::AutoScalingGroup
    properties:
      min_size: 2
      max_size: 5
      resource:
        type: web-server.yaml
        properties:
          pool_id: {get_resource: pool}
          network: {get_param: network}
          parent_stack_id: {get_param: "OS::stack_id"}
  scaleup_policy:
    type: OS::Heat::ScalingPolicy
    properties:
      adjustment_type: change_in_capacity
      auto_scaling_group_id: {get_resource: web_server_group}
      cooldown: 30
      scaling_adjustment: 1
  scaledown_policy:
    type: OS::Heat::ScalingPolicy
    properties:
      adjustment_type: change_in_capacity
      auto_scaling_group_id: {get_resource: web_server_group}
```

```
     cooldown: 30
     scaling_adjustment: -1
 cpu_alarm_high:
  type: OS::Ceilometer::Alarm
  properties:
   description: If the avg CPU > 40% for 30 seconds then scale up
   meter_name: cpu_util
   statistic: avg
   period: 30
   evaluation_periods: 1
   threshold: 40
   alarm_actions:
    - {get_attr: [scaleup_policy, alarm_url]}
   matching_metadata: {'metadata.user_metadata.stack': {get_param: "OS::stack_id"}}
   comparison_operator: gt
 cpu_alarm_low:
  type: OS::Ceilometer::Alarm
  properties:
   description: If the avg CPU < 15% for 90 seconds then scale down
   meter_name: cpu_util
   statistic: avg
   period: 90
   evaluation_periods: 1
   threshold: 15
   alarm_actions:
    - {get_attr: [scaledown_policy, alarm_url]}
   matching_metadata: {'metadata.user_metadata.stack': {get_param: "OS::stack_id"}}
   comparison_operator: lt
 monitor:
  type: OS::Neutron::HealthMonitor
  properties:
   type: TCP
   delay: 5
   max_retries: 5
   timeout: 5
 pool:
  type: OS::Neutron::Pool
  properties:
   protocol: HTTP
   monitors: [{get_resource: monitor}]
   subnet_id: {get_param: subnet_id}
   lb_method: ROUND_ROBIN
   vip:
    protocol_port: 80
 lb:
  type: OS::Neutron::LoadBalancer
  properties:
   protocol_port: 80
   pool_id: {get_resource: pool}

 lb_floating:
  type: OS::Neutron::FloatingIP
  properties:
   floating_network_id: {get_param: external_network_id}
   port_id: {get_attr: [pool, vip, port_id]}
```

```
outputs:
 scale_up_url:
  description: >
   Invoke the scale-up operation by doing an HTTP POST to this
   URL;
  value: {get_attr: [scaleup_policy, alarm_url]}
 scale_dn_url:
  description: >
   Invoke the scale-down operation by doing an HTTP POST to
   this URL;
  value: {get_attr: [scaledown_policy, alarm_url]}
 pool_ip_address:
  value: {get_attr: [pool, vip, address]}
  description: The IP address of the load balancing pool
 website_url:
  value:
   str_replace:
    template: http://host/
    params:
     host: { get_attr: [lb_floating, floating_ip_address] }
  description: >
   This URL is the "external" load balanced url
```

Let's call this file `final.yaml`. It contains all of the necessary instructions to create multiple servers as defined by the `web-server.yaml` file. It will maintain a minimum of two of these servers, and scale up to a maximum of five as defined by the min and max size of the auto-scaling group. It also implements the Ceilometer alarms that trigger scaling up when a CPU average goes above 40 percent for 30 seconds, trigger scaling down when CPU average goes below 15 percent for 90 seconds, and applies these alarms to the sever group as policies.

To create/update a stack with this template you would first need to manually create a network, subnet, and router for the servers/load balancer. You would then pass these values in as parameters like this:

```
$ heat stack-create -f final.yaml -P "network=web-net;subnet_id=$subnet_id; ↵
    external_network_id=$public_net_id" autoscale;
```

That should output a number of things including the web address of the load balancer that will round robin to the two web servers. Hitting that URL repeatedly should display the various IP addresses of the provisioned servers in round robin fashion. After a short period of time, new servers should be added and new addresses will appear, then as load decreases they should disappear. If you want to try this for yourself, these templates along with a script to create the necessary networks are available in the `final_deployment` folder of the GitHub repo for this book at: `https://github.com/johnbelamaric/openstack-appdev-book`.

To use this method to deploy our demo application, we would use a combination of two AutoScalingGroups (one for the web and one for the API tier), and a ResourceGroup for the MySQL tier. The `user_data` portion of each group would then contain the configuration commands for that server type and each group could be scaled independently. Scripts like this generally take a lot longer to create than it would to manually provision and configure an environment one time. Hopefully though, you can now see the advantage here of being able to programmatically recreate everything an application needs at the push of a button. If a project was to be wiped out, or a dev/test area needed, another environment could be instantly created and put to work.

This is not a one size fits all solution. The choices made were all based on personal preference, ease of use, and the requirements of the demo application and environment. There are many other options, and when deploying your own cloud application, your final solution will likely involve different choices and look vastly different. This is to be expected. Hopefully though, you now have the basic knowledge and skills to make those choices, and script the deployment of your own cloud based application.

UPDATING AND PATCHING

There are times when you will deploy an application and your work is essentially done. Applications will often keep themselves up to date via automatic update. Modern browsers are a good example of this. Many of them simply check for an update on startup, download the patch and apply it before starting. Often though, applications have a number of components that need to be manually updated quite frequently. The jQuery library within many web based application is a good example of this. The servers themselves may also need to be patched. Security updates for exploits, and fixes that improve performance are both commonplace in any company.

At first, it may seem like the traditional methods should simply be employed here, and they can be. Manually updating, and rebooting servers will definitely patch them. Any standard methodology for promoting code changes will also work. Once deployed, an OpenStack backed application is comparable for the most part to one living in a hardware only world.

The minimal cost of deploying new servers, though, and the ability to programmatically script networking allows for some unique ways handle on-going maintenance.

Patching Options

If you work within a larger corporate structure, it's likely that some kind of patching mechanism already exists for you. Allowing even a few machines on a network to be compromised due to missing security updates is a real world problem. Even if you are in this situation however, it's unlikely that all of your patching will be taken care of by this means. Patches for specialized software for your application and updates that don't address a performance or security issue are often still the responsibility of devops.

One option for patching depends on your configuration management choice. If you opted to use third party tools like Puppet or Chef, their centralized administrative features can make patching a breeze. They both allow for scheduled updates, and as was mentioned earlier, remote execution. If you designed your application with multiple regions or multiple load-balanced clusters as discussed in Chapter 5, it should be a simple matter to patch/reboot one region/cluster at a time and avoid any down time.

Ansible's remote execution ability can be a solid solution here as well. Your application will likely contain many small servers. You can group these into arbitrary sets in an Ansible configuration file and then execute update commands on one group at a time. This is a good way to avoid both down-time and the need to re-provision all together.

OpenStack doesn't provide any specific first party tools for patching. Instead, the components we have already discussed can be used and Glance/Images are another common avenue for patching. Though still not recommended as a complete solution, updated images are frequently available and can be used to handle basic OS updates. To bring a system to compliance, an application can simply be re-deployed in part or in total with these new images.

This would be a great reason to include the image as a parameter in your Heat template. Running the following command could then update all of the servers with this new image:

```
$ heat stack-update test_stack -f test.yaml -P "image=CentOS64-Update2"
```

Of course this may re-provision all of your servers at once, so even if you don't have multiple logical clusters, it might be useful to split your servers into different ResourceGroups solely for patching purposes. This way it's possible to change the image on just one group at a time:

```
$ heat stack-update test_stack -f test.yaml -P "group1_image=CentOS ↵
    64-Update2;group2_image=CentOS64-Update3"
```

CI/CD in an OpenStack World

No modern text for developers (or devops) would be complete without at least some mention of agile methodology. Its tenants are pervasive in the modern workplace and technical community. The need to frequently release updates, to A/B test, and to programmatically test the codebase of an application as part of a deployment are all challenging aspects of CI/CD (Continuous Integration/Continuous Delivery) and agile philosophy in any type of environment. Fortunately, with OpenStack, your deployment solution can actually provide some unique solutions to these challenges. Let's look at these one at a time.

The first requirement here is for frequent releases. If you are migrating an application to the cloud, then in all likelihood your current mechanism for updating production code will continue to work. This can be handled in all of the same manners discussed previously for patching. Once an application has passed all of its tests, it is a just a matter of contacting any of OpenStack's APIs such as Heat or Nova to provision new servers and tear down the old ones. If containers are your virtualization technology of choice, you will almost certainly be deploying all of your changes in this manner. If not, then Ansible or similar technology can also be used remotely execute commands on batches of servers to update code from a central repository.

OpenStack presents the next challenge with more intriguing solutions. The need to A/B test can be integral to making informed choices in an application's evolution. Traditional methods of handling this include buckets, where an application runs several different versions on the same machine, or code based solutions that programmatically present different options to different users. The ability to actually duplicate portions of your production environment, however, can allow you to quickly deploy multiple versions of the application simultaneously. This provides a complete separation of the codebase A from codebase B, allowing performance comparisons and preventing one codebase from crashing the other. Once the test is concluded, A or B can then be torn down and those resources dedicated to other projects.

The last item, application testing, which usually includes unit as well as functional tests, also has some unique solutions in a cloud-based world. Unit tests can be run just about anywhere, but functional tests often require a fully functional environment. This is another opportunity to use your deployment script to create another working environment to run these tests in. It's reasonable to picture a system where a commit hook sets off a call to create an environment, tests are run, results are published, and the environment is then torn down. Using your deployment script, template, or whatever technology chosen, ensures that this test environment can perfectly mimic the production environment and is never affected by previous tests. It's even possible in this scenario for multiple test environments to be running multiple versions of the application and its tests, as opposed to waiting in a queue for a single dedicated test environment.

In general, OpenStack should make both CI/CD and patching much easier, or at least present a whole host of solutions that were unavailable before. Many of these solutions aren't specific to OpenStack and are available within any cloud environment. However, your deployment solution will likely be very OpenStack specific, and will impact how you go about patching and updating your application/environment. It is for that reason that this chapter is concluded with this discussion on maintenance. It is one last thing to consider before settling on a final deployment solution.

SUMMARY

If you have been in the role of a developer or a system administrator, making all of the necessary choices and scripting them can be a big shift. Bridging these two worlds comes with a lot of benefit though, and it is likely to be the way things move going forward, since these benefits often arise in the form of huge cost savings. There is current demand for devops expertise for this reason. While the deployment of containers and third-party development will continue to evolve, the fundamental concept of provisioning your hardware and networking, along with your software, is here to stay in one form or another. The fact that OpenStack tries to provide an open-ended platform for these concepts to flourish, makes it a great choice regardless of which technologies end up winning in the end.

BOOK WRAP UP

In this book we have discussed exactly what OpenStack is and what it provides. The various components and projects that comprise the bulk of OpenStack have been described. Examples of how to create and improve applications using some of the unique aspects of the cloud have been covered. We have also provided options for deploying and maintaining these applications, all of which will help you get started using OpenStack.

One of the great joys of working within an OpenStack backed environment is the ability to experiment without consequence. You can lock up a server and reboot it from a website without calling down to the server room. You can allocate and de-allocate assets like drive space, IP addresses and databases without the frustration of service tickets. Even misconfiguring a server to the point where it is unusable, can be fixed by deleting and re-provisioning it in seconds. This kind of self-service infrastructure is at the heart of the devops movement and makes learning OpenStack fun and exciting. It can also make it a little overwhelming.

The sheer breadth of what can be accomplished using OpenStack is a bit daunting. It's more than just another program to use or another language with yet another way of writing if then statements. OpenStack and other cloud-based solutions represent a fundamental shift in how the web is created, and how modern web-based applications are designed. It requires a completely new skillset as well as the ability to think of previously physical objects like servers, and networking equipment as objects in a software program. Even the names of these things themselves can get overwhelming. Sorting out the Nova's, Neutrons, Kilos, and Kubernetes takes both time and dedication as well as some interest in the subject.

For some, this may come naturally, but for most of us it takes a lot of experimentation, failure, and well…more failure. Mastery comes with its own rewards, and in the case of OpenStack, it can allow you to do things that you have wanted to do for years and give you control over your environment in a way that you have never had before.

In addition to this book, there are a number of resources to help you gain this mastery. First and foremost, the web is full of tutorials, blogs, and API documentation for OpenStack. Some sites you might find useful in your journey:

➤ `https://www.openstack.org/`: The central hub for all things OpenStack, and worth exploring even if you're not looking for an answer to a specific question.

➤ `http://developer.openstack.org/api-ref.html`: One of several API references available. It always seems to be missing a few things, but is updated frequently and is probably your best bet for API documentation and examples.

➤ `https://developer.rackspace.com/blog/`: Rackspace continues to provide great up to date tutorials and interesting discussions on all topics OpenStack.

➤ `https://wiki.openstack.org`: Covers great descriptions of all of the major projects, and is a good place to start if you want to dig deeper into any individual component.

If you want to go beyond the web, more and more classes and physical world resources are becoming available as OpenStack adoption increases. Another major avenue to increase your OpenStack knowledge and expertise might be one of the semi-annual conferences held all over the world. You can see where these are being held at: `https://www.openstack.org/summit/`.

Sharing your experiences with OpenStack and participating in the community is also a great gateway of actually contributing to OpenStack. This can be as simple as providing documentation on a missing method or value, or as complex as providing a patch for the next major release. Exactly how much you want to get involved is up to you, but doing so can be rewarding and is an exciting part of what it means to utilize open source software.

In the end, OpenStack is about choice: the choice of how to implement it, the choice of how to use it, and the choice of how to participate in its lifecycle. This, more than anything else, is what makes OpenStack a unique offering in a surprisingly crowded field. Now go and use OpenStack to build the next great success story!

INDEX